Psychology

DESIGNING THE DISCIPLINE

Joseph Margolis
Peter T. Manicas
Rom Harré
Paul F. Secord

Basil Blackwell

© Joseph Margolis, Peter T. Manicas, Rom Harré, Paul F. Secord 1986

First published 1986

Basil Blackwell Ltd
108 Cowley Road, Oxford OX4 1JF, UK

Basil Blackwell Inc.
432 Park Avenue South, Suite 1503,
New York, NY 10016, USA

British Library Cataloguing in Publication Data

Psychology: designing the discipline.
1. Psychology – Philosophy
1. Margolis, Joseph
150'.1 BF38
ISBN 0-631-14998-8

Library of Congress Cataloging in Publication Data

Psychology, designing the discipline.

Includes index.
1. Psychology — Philosophy.   I. Margolis, Joseph Zalman, 1924–
BF38.P787   1986   150'.1   86–9694
ISBN 0-631-14998-8

Typeset by Alan Sutton Publishing Limited
Printed in Great Britain by Billings Ltd, Worcester

Contents

Preface

The four of us shared a symposium on the state of the art, at the American Psychological Association meetings in Toronto in August 1984. Paul Secord had taken the initiative. We hadn't expected our separate presentations to fit together as well as they did, but the natural unity they signified and the enthusiasm of our professional audience led spontaneously to planning this volume. We had the distinct impression that many in the various subdisciplines of psychology were rather strongly drawn in our direction, and have tried here to give a sense of the rationale for this new turn from a variety of perspectives. Hopefully, an occasion will arise to pursue all the essential themes in the full and rigorous way they deserve.

Joseph Margolis
Peter T. Manicas
Rom Harré
Paul F. Secord

1

Introduction

Paul F. Secord and Joseph Margolis

This book addresses the question of the extent to which psychology is an autonomous science. Although the question is an old one, it is asked here in a sharper, more focused way. It was not until the twentieth century that psychology emerged as an apparently autonomous science. Before the late nineteenth century, psychology was typically a branch of philosophy and although in this century it has established strong claims to being an independent science, it is occasionally challenged by other disciplines ranging from biology to the social sciences as well as by new developments in the history and philosophy of science. The issue may be more sharply formulated along two lines:

1 Are the characteristic phenomena of psychology explained in terms of vocabularies and explanatory models that are more or less restricted to what are usually regarded as psychological factors, or are they (or must they be) explained in both multi-directional and multi-level ways: for instance, in terms of physical, chemical, biochemical, neurological, psychological and social factors?

2 Is psychology reducible or emergent (non-reducible) as a science *vis-à-vis* the physical or biological or information sciences; that is, are the distinctive factors and explanatory models of psychology either effectively expressible as or replaceable by factors and models that belong to the physical, biological, information or similar domains?

The automony question has currently taken on special significance because of developments in the entire range of the sciences and of disciplined inquiry. These developments, especially those centering around psychology, pose a strenuous challenge to programs of reductionism and to the unity of science theme. In particular, emphasis in the physical sciences on the history and actual practice of science has raised doubts about the conceptual adequacy of standard models of the descriptive and explanatory structure of just those paradigm sciences. Gains in the biological and information sciences have encouraged new notions of how to characterize the distinction of psychology: for instance, along the lines of what are usually called the cognitive sciences. The increasingly close linkage between psychology and the social sciences, which for their own part exhibit somewhat opposed tendencies regarding reduction and the like, have focused the issue of autonomy in a dramatic way. These converging developments oblige methodologically concerned professionals to reconsider the state of psychology; the double question of its autonomy is, therefore, particularly central to any responsible canvass of the conceptual structure of an entire family of interrelated disciplines, although our concern focuses primarily on psychology.

This book will provide an overview of the principal issues bearing on the fairly technical question of autonomy. That question requires at the very least a careful treatment of issues arising chiefly in the professional work of the various subdisciplines within empirical psychology and in the somewhat more abstract concerns of philosophers of science. Psychology is at a most important crossroads; lively developments in both psychology and philosophy as well as in the informational and social sciences demand a fresh overview of its conceptual standing. The new line goes beyond mere reaction to the strong reductionism, physicalism, and extensionalism that have so frequently surfaced in Anglo-American accounts of the sciences; it means to challenge in a critical and sustained way the claims of those who have been most sanguine about and most influential in pressing the advantages of reductionism and the unity of science program. Furthermore, in being thus committed, the new line explicitly recognizes the important sense in which we cannot escape adjusting the theory of what psychology is about to its actual empirical work and at the same time (a matter often ignored) adjusting the direction and even small-gauge work of psychology in accordance with our theories of the best promise and the most reasonable picture of the discipline we can muster. Fashionably nowadays, philosophers are fond of supposing (quite mistakenly) that the sciences can pursue their own 'first order' inquiries without raising any 'second order' questions about the very legitimacy of practicing as they do. And psychologists are often quite content to pursue their programs and inquiries without bothering to theorize in the philosophical spirit, even if that means acknowledging a certain partisan loyalty in what they thus favor. A sense of inexorable historical change and of plural options beckoning at every phase of such change should persuade us of the unreasonbleness of such disjunctions.

Until very recently, for example, the *sui generis* peculiarities of language, societal training, institutions, social history, the relation between the genetic endowment of the human race and the cultural variations that may exploit that common endowment, the complexities of mental life, the linkage between human individuals and social ensembles, cognitive development and social learning have all been distinctly subordinated to the older requirements of the favored unity of science program. All that is changing; yet, there is no substitute program that offers a comparably balanced or clearcut conceptual picture of professional psychology as it is taking shape at present and as it is bound to develop in the near future. Our plan is to provide an overview of the issues for such a program and thus to fill a need that many now acknowledge. The chapter by Margolis provides an overall view of the complex issues involved in the double question of psychology's autonomy as seen from the perspective of the philosophy of science. He argues that science and philosophy are linked in an intimate way and that this link has a special bearing on psychology. For if psychology is accepted as a science, then extraordinary difficulties arise for logical empiricism and its family of close successors, which for most of the twentieth century have formed the dominant view of science. Rudolf Carnap's early view – that physical language is a universal language into which every factual sentence can be translated – proved untenable for both observational and high-level theoretical statements. Carnap himself relented of course. Eventually, weaker extensionalist views were advanced in a deliberate effort to save the unity of science program. For example, it was argued that, in emergent domains like biology and psychology, laws need not actually be translated into physicalistic statements, but certain close congruities must obtain between such laws and exemplary physical laws, both with regard to logical form and vocabulary.

Margolis observes that psychology is a particularly crucial test of physicalism, for it seems impossible to pursue science without relying on the entire conceptual network and experience that shape our very ability to pursue our inquiries. In a fair sense, though for other purposes, the influential American philosopher, Willard Quine, has insisted on the same point. That means that one cannot escape reference to subjective experiences, introspective reports, shifting and largely tacit conceptual networks, in spite of the fact that the very role of the scientist advancing his discipline must be subject to the same explanatory work as the phenomenon he studies. Describing the activities of scientists appears to intrude peculiarly objectionable terms (intentions, interpretations of meaning, etc.) that the unity program had meant to eliminate. These points are obscured when the psychologist is content to conform with the merely formal features of extensionalism and to ignore the complexities of his or her actual practice.

The extensionalist model may be read either as a largely apt if somewhat idealized account or as a frankly exteme, limiting, essentially unattainable objective. Favoring the second view, Margolis observes that even if, within certain constraints, portions of psychological phenomena can be fitted to the extensionalist view, the unity of science program still fails if critics are able to establish that central ranges of phenomena and certain central questions have not been and seem not in principle to be fully capable of supporting that view. But the extensionalist view cannot and need not be shown to be wrong utterly and unconditionally, when applied to psychology.

Margolis notes that since cognitive states cannot be ignored, psychology centres on human psychology. This acknowledgement creates great difficulties for physicalist and extensionalist views. No one has succeeded in reducing cognitive states to physical states or in providing a thoroughly extensionalist analysis of cognition. Several reduction strategies that might eliminate intentionality have been attempted. Margolis discusses these moves and their limitations.

The role of intentionality in psychology goes back to Franz Brentano and has been pursued by a number of noted psychologists, including Wilhelm Wundt. Intentionality highlights the complexity of cognitive states; its statements are peculiar because the verbs 'refer' to the object of the sentence in a different way from nonintentional statements. One cannot say in truth (unless to convey one's intention), '*I shot* a unicorn'; but one can truthfully say 'I am *thinking* about a unicorn'. What purport to be the objects of sentences reporting or describing intentional states can be fictional or non-existent, but that is impossible where transitive verbs designate physical or causal processes. Sentences about intentional phenomena often behave intensionally, that is, non-extensionally. But discourse about the physical is said to behave extensionally.

Intensionality, then, is a direct challenge to physicalism and the doctrine of extensionality. Proponents of extensionality hoped to eliminate intensionality as a feature of whatever might be the real phenomena of psychology by eliminating or neutralizing intentionality appropriately. But the intensional complexity of intentionality extends to language, history, social practice and the like. To treat these phenomena as real is to set a considerable hurdle for the champions of extensionality and the unity of science program to surmount.

Margolis raises two puzzles: emergence and methodological individualism. (1) Although human language presumably emerged from sub-human life forms human language appears not to be explicable as purely physical or sub-linguistic processes; (2) Humans are effective agents; yet languages, institutions and the like are not explicable merely in terms of individual human agency. Accepting strong versions of (1) and (2) threatens extensionalism and the unity of science program – if it does not render them impossible. Moreover it follows that psychology cannot be autonomous. Margolis goes on to note that all sciences are human enterprises and that no physicalist reduction of science has ever been achieved. At best, if the form of explanation in psychology can be applied to lower levels (by analogy, for example, to non-human animals), a kind of unity, much weaker, logically, than the unity of science program favors, might be achieved, based on the top-down explanations of psychology and the human sciences. This may be the only way in which science itself can be scientifically explained. In effect, the enterprise of science itself is a salient phenomenon of human psychology.

Margolis calls attention to two views of natural language. On one, natural languages are treated as fundamentally governed by formal, asocial structures largely prior to history and social interaction. On the other, language, traditions, social practices and the like are features abstracted from the life of entire societies. Explanations of human action must, therefore, deal with this complication as well as mere individual agency. Although extreme individualism as well as extreme holism must be avoided, the human sciences must deal with both polarities if they are to be adequate to the task. Chomsky and Fodor favor the first extreme, treating language largely as formal and asocial; they hope thereby to redeem part of the unity of science model, by proposing a genetically innate 'language' in accord with which natural languages develop and without which they would (they claim) remain inexplicable. But there appear to be other, less counterintuitive, options.

Margolis considers how 'top-down' and 'bottom-up' psychologies deal with the puzzles so far raised. Bottom-up psychologies are those patterned after the physical sciences, while top-down psychologies would start with the emergent features of human language and culture and work down through the different strata. Bottom-up strategies start with simple elements and compose more complex orders at higher and higher levels of organization. They are compositional and hierarchical in principle. Top-down strategies are factorial, starting with more holistic, emergent, and molar phenomena. Margolis considers a variety of strategies of both kinds and discusses their advantages and limitations. For example, some bottom-up strategies would simply eliminate the problems raised by intentionality, in order to maintain the extensionalist view of science. Some recent bottom-up strategies have departed from a traditional version of physicialism, assuming informational elements as basic and (perhaps) non-reducible, on which an informational hierarchy may be constructed. But since information is normally represented propositionally – and thus is linguistically modelled – it is unclear what is the nature of those bottom-up strategies that posit fundamental informational elements.

Strategies of these latter sorts converge on functionalism, which 'isolates an intentional, teleological, informational, coded, semiotic, or similar set of abstract traits assignable in psychological or cognitive contexts, that are distinct from physical or biological traits and that are not reducible to the latter.' That line of thought both threatens a new dualism and ignores the matrix of societal life in which, particularly, the phenomena thus characterized are salient. The countermeasures required seem to indicate that the functional must be incarnate in the biological and psychological, must be abstracted only in a top-down manner, and must be drawn from societal practices that the aptitudes of individual human agents manifest. But to say that is to oppose the autonomy of the science of psychology.

In chapter 3, Manicas argues that, to the extent that psychology can be a science, it is limited to the study of human competencies such as learning, perception and memory rather than extended to the study of behavior in life settings. Close attention must be paid to Manicas's arguments, for his conclusions are so foreign to psychologists' thinking that they tend to be rejected out of hand. This can be seen when his claim is put in the tersest possible way: psychology is *not* the business of explaining behavior. He asserts that the premise that psychologists could explain behavior is based on two assumptions that are demonstrably false: (1) behavior can be conceptualized and studied at a psychological level which does not involve social contexts or social relations, and (2) behavior can be reduced to biological terms.

Manicas sees the biological organism as an ordered set of complex systems. The various levels – marked in terms of cells, organs, and the like – appear as emergent within inquiry, but no one grasps the interlocking complex of all its relations. A vital feature of complex organisms is that properties emerge at different 'levels' and cannot be derived from a knowledge of the elements of lower levels alone.

Moreover, some higher-level properties have causal effects on how 'elements' at lower levels function. There is in fact evidence of interlevel causality. Movements of the whole organism, for example, can result in survival or death.

Particularly significant for psychology is the point that 'persons are culturally emergent in the sense that they have distinctive capacities (actual properties – for instance, linguistic abilities) predicable of them only in virtue of the causal outcomes of their biological development within a peculiarly complex social environment'. Psychology cannot be reduced to biology. Insofar as one's behavior can be affected by another's speech, meaningful speech is emergent, not reducible, and causally efficacious at a psychological level. Persons, then, have casual powers stemming from their biology, but not reducible to that biology. This realist view differs sharply from those functional theories favored in cognitive psychology and artificial intelligence that equate the abstract or formal properties of a machine (say, a thinking computer) with the intelligence of a human organism (a thinking person): the flesh and blood of the living organism are fully implicated in its psychological capacities, which the merely formal resemblance to a computer fails to explain because its capacities are radically different, not abstract at all.

Seen in this light, Manicas continues, the business of psychology is not the explanation of behavior, but the explanation of capacities: perception, learning, and the like. Moreover, these capacities cannot be explained solely on the psychological level; the role of the biological properties of the organism in generating these capacities must be considered.

Two questions remain. Can human action be explained in terms of individual behaviors, or must societal facts be invoked? Second, is there a level at which the psychological properties of persons (or individual humans) are distinct from the social?

Disputes between methodological individualism and holism *vis-à-vis* explanations in the social sciences have been pursued for years. As Manicas notes, methodological individualism raises the question of whether a nonsocial (strictly individualistic) explanation can be given of human behavior. There is growing agreement from many quarters that the answer is no. The strongest argument is that behavior is language-impregnated, and thus any explanation must appeal to irreducible social predicates. This is entailed by the fact that language is a societal structure, in some sense pre-existing individuals, although only individuals actually speak.

For this reason behavior cannot be explained solely in psychological terms, where 'psychological' signifies properties applicable only to individuals. But this does not eliminate psychology. Manicas identifies an infrapsychological level which he sees as the proper province of psychology. At this level, psychologists would work to discover the causal mechanisms of perception, cognition, memory and learning which provide us with the initial capacities we use to function in our social world. But note that casual processes work both ways: these underlying biological processes are linked to the social world through the capacities they endow us with; thus, the social world can affect the manner in which neurological mechanisms operate.

In chapter 4, Harré further undermines the thesis that psychology is autonomous by demonstrating the profoundly intimate way in which language and society pervade psychological processes. Many aspects of the psychology of individuals are the products of social processes: the repertoire of emotions, the organization of one's thoughts, and the self. Individuality, according to Harré, is an illusion. Human rationality is not an individual phenomenon, but must be understood in terms of social conventions. Even making a moral decision is often the outcome of public conversations rather than of isolated individuals making up their minds.

Building on J. L. Austin's views of speech acts, Harré develops a notion of conversation as embodying a moral order. Speech acts are social acts and their meaning depends upon particular occasions of utterance. Like the ethnomethodologists (see chapter 5) Harré argues that speech acts are only fully understood when their indexicalities are grasped: the referents of 'where', 'when', 'who' and 'what' must come to be known. But further, speech acts take place in a 'people-space', which involves an unequal distribution of rights, obligations, and duties that, together, constitute a moral order. Thus the profound link between individual action and the social order is reflected in the fact that conversational practices themselves have a moral import.

Associated with the moral order are criteria for the evaluation of actions and the worth of people. These structure people-space to control the kinds of speech acts that may flow through any space. Behind speech practices is a system of beliefs and conventions; here, Harré differs from the ethnomethodologists, who would argue that beliefs and conventions are located only in the conversation itself, do not extend beyond local practical actions. Harré illustrates his thesis by showing how it applies to the self and to emotions.

Both the emotions and the self involve 'a dialectical reciprocity between the individual and the collective aspects of psychological functioning along the boundary between the psychological research area and the sociological'. This has at least two consequences: (1) there is no such thing as universal emotions native to all humans; instead, emotions are generated from physiological arousal in culturally diverse ways, reflecting the influence of different vocabularies and different moral orders; (2) persons develop feelings and generate predicates about themselves in a manner ordered by grammatical models and moral orders; the very unity of the self is generated by society itself and takes a form appropriate to the culture of that society.

Emotions are not responses suffered by passive participants, nor are there a small number of basic emotions; the local social world shapes emotions in an infinite variety of ways. Local moral orders promote very different emotions in different cultures. All emotions are *intentional* in that they are about something: we are 'afraid of, mad at, proud of, or grieving for'.

Both individuals and collectives are created by structuration: a process whereby the boundary between the personal and the social is crossed and recrossed: the people-makers of a culture help to synthesize the self. Because of the social nature of the self, persons are as morally responsible for their private thoughts as for their public ones. Finally, Harré postulates two 'orthogonal' dimensions: public/private and individual/collective, which create four domains that systematically characterize the various ways in which persons and society intersect.

In the final chapter, Secord examines *social* psychology, a subdiscipline of psychology and of sociology, from the philosphical perspectives central to this book. At least four distinct social psychologies are identified: a social psychology emergent from the parent discipline of psychology itself, and three subdisciplines that emerge from sociology – symbolic interactionism, psychological sociology, and ethnomethodology. For each subdiscipline, Secord traces the origins of its paradigmatic features to the philosophical characteristics of the parent discipline, which include positions taken on two polarities: individual/social and inner/outer.

Secord ties the individual/social polarity closely to the familiar dispute between methodological individualism and holism: most psychologists believe that full explanations of behavior can be provided by an understanding of individual mechanisms of behavior and, surprisingly, even many psychologically trained social psycholgists subscribe to such beliefs. This bias is reflected in the centrality of such concepts as attitude, cognitive consistency, dissonance and attribution, and by the warm reception given to the vigorous cognitive science movement in general psychology. As might be expected, training in sociology produces a bias in the opposite direction, toward interactions and collectivities instead of individuals.

Perhaps even more striking is the position of psychologists on the inner/outer polarity. Psychology is believed to be about the mind and mental (cognitive/affective) processes; again, psychologically trained social psychologists have spent most of their efforts attempting to explain social behavior in comparable terms while ignoring external structures and processes. In contrast, none of the three sociologically-oriented social psychologies gives a central place to mental processes. Language, for example, is usually seen as a socially generated product in accord with which human action is characterized in ways 'external' to the individual person.

Because of their concern with the *social* it might be thought that these four subdisciplines could have escaped the constraints of logical positivism/empiricism; but Secord notes this did not happen in the case of psychological social psychology or even, entirely, in the case of psychological sociology. Both symbolic interactionism and ethnomethodology, however, place great emphasis on language and meaning; ethnomethodology in particular offers powerful arguments to the effect that human behavior is inescapably social and linguistic, thus supporting the position that psychology cannot be autonomous. Indeed, ethnomethodology goes so far in the direction of viewing human action as a practical accomplishment indigenous to the situations in which it occurs that the question arises as to whether anything resembling a science can emerge from this subdiscipline. At the same time, its positive contribution lies in its critique of psychological/sociological approaches that attempt to follow positivist/empiricist constraints and thereby produce forms of research prone to favor highly abstract variables that often poorly represent the human action that presumably is the actual object of study.

Finally, Secord calls attention to the fact that none of the social pyschologies adequately relates individual behavior to the societal contexts and structures in which it occurs. Macrostructures, such as institutions and other organizations, as well as cultural and demographic attributes, constrain, facilitate, and in other ways affect individual behavior in unrecognized respects. Taken together, symbolic interactionism and ethnomethodology, along with several other closely related movements such as ethogeny (see Harré, this volume), social constructivism, dialectics, and hermeneutics offer a powerful critique of social psychology as it has been practiced in the past. But Secord concludes that, to be successful, a future social psychology must be interdisciplinary and, moreover, must transcend competing paradigms by developing a theory than can embrace them despite their mutual tensions and apparent incongruences.

Reviewing matters once again, more globally, we say that the autonomy of a science is usually estimated – both intuitively and with precision – in terms, (1) of the explanatory power of the covering laws that may be formulated within the domain that it specifies as its own, or (2) of the explanatory power of the processes or mechanisms that may be specified within the space of that same domain. If one insists that (1) or (2) must be construed as providing a fully sufficient account of pertinent phenomena (on some model of explanation), then very likely no science is autonomous – or at any rate none are competent in all domains. But if one construes explanation in terms of necessary rather than sufficient criteria, then interest in the autonomy of psychology is at least a reasonable concern. Under such an accommodation, arguments regarding the linkage between psychology and the biological and the social sciences bear in a productive way on the issue at stake. So seen, the four accounts that follow oppose the autonomy thesis.

They are not entirely in agreement with one another on all counts. But they are strongly convergent on the dependant standing of psychology as a science. That is the important fact. The theme of autonomy has, it may be claimed, two principal foci: one, that the phenomena of psychology are such that the laws or mechanisms appealed to in explanatory contexts are essentially functional – that is to say, abstractable from more fundamental biological structures within which psychological phenomena surely manifest themselves; the other, that societal settings are rightly seen as supplying only the referential contexts within which the psychological appears, rather than as collecting any properties or forces that are essential elements of the psychological itself. These are the alternatives reviewed in what follows. Our purpose, then, is to give psychology a strong new direction, not to insist on any menu of detailed doctrines. The essays that follow are, then, exemplars – from four different points of view and with an eye to four different aspects of the central question – of how the denial of the autonomy thesis may be fruitfully elaborated.

2

Psychology and Its Methodological Options

Joseph Margolis

The question of being a science

It is very common to speak of psychology as a science; and yet, when its credentials are examined, it is not entirely clear whether it is a science or whether, granting that it is a science, our picture is clear of what a science is. The point of hesitation is a familiar one, which, pressed a little more insistently, signifies the indissoluble connection between practicing a science and theorizing about what concerning such practice justifies its characterization as a science. This is a disputed matter, frankly, but nearly all of the most commanding views of science concede the implausibility of any strong disjunction between pursuing the (so-called first-order) work of an empirical science and (so-called second-order) philosophical reflections about the cognitive powers or legitimacy of any first-order discipline.

The reason the issue is not merely a verbal nicety is that there are very good grounds for supposing that our conception of what constitutes a science affects in a substantive way - though perhaps tacitly, by the imperceptible preformation of our sense of disciplined inquiry, by being the creatures of history that we are, by the informality with which we usually reflect on such matters – how we actually formulate and pursue the questions of any would-be science. There are also good grounds for believing that our pertinent practices – inevitably local, contingently favored, loosely linked with other allegedly scientific practices and even possibly opposed to the methods they favor – substantively affect our theory of what a science is. The symbiosis and inevitable equilibration between the two are entirely natural, neither lightly nor cynically to be dismissed. For it is not in the least clear that there is any source of relief, and it is not at all certain that that condition vitiates either the admirable work of what we call the sciences or the reasonableness of trying to form the best possible picture, under the circumstances, of what we take a science to be.

Surely, in physics, if we but consider the work of Boltzmann, Einstein, Planck, Bohr and Heisenberg, it is quite impossible to segregate the scientific and philosophical ingredients of their respective views leading to and developing relativity and quantum physics, or to assess which such ingredients were the most decisive in vindicating their own results. In the more narrow confines of the philosophy of science, it is certainly clear in the work of Popper, Kuhn, Lakatos, Feyerabend and others that the persuasiveness of high-level theories and the directions of supposedly promising avenues of research are functions of background theories and conceptual orientation that could not possibly be made to rest on a strongly disjunctive reading of science and philosophy. In fact, in one of the most celebrated short papers of analytic philosophy, W. V. Quine's 'Two dogmas of empiricism' (1953), a powerful argument is advanced according to which there are no convincing grounds for segregating in a principled way questions of meaning and questions of belief or, alternatively, for contrasting analytic and synthetic truths (presumably, what a contrast between philosophy and science would require).

The reason for insisting on the point bears directly on the fortune of psychology. Because in our recent past, in the twenties and thirties, when the principal papers of Einstein and Planck had already been published and required reconciliation with an adequate model of science, there was developed, particularly through the so-called Vienna Circle, largely led in accord with the somewhat different convictions of Moritz Schlick and Rudolf Carnap, a conception of what it is to be a science, that formed the principal inspiration for the so-called unity of science movement (more through Carnap's efforts than through Schlick's). As it happens, that vision was succinctly formulated by Carnap in the context of specifying the very sense in which psychology was and was rightly regarded as a science – a discipline falling within the unity of science program. And, ironically, it was the conceptual foundations of that vision that Quine completely undermined in the paper mentioned – without, however, intending to discourage the conception or pursuit of psychology (or of any other would-be science) along the general lines that Carnap outlined. Furthermore, this general vision of science must be counted as the most up-to-date and most informed systematic conception ever formulated, since it follows the pioneer studies of relativity and quantum physics, which dominate our century's physics, and since no alternative philosophical conception of comparable power has as yet been formulated, following what can only be called its near-collapse. The point is that nearly every serious effort in our century to characterize the science of psychology has been strongly influenced, if not entirely led, by the norms and ideals of Carnap's vision or of the variously modified versions of the unity of science program that have branched out from or anticipated it or converged with it (see Causey, 1977; Neurath et al., 1955, vol. 1; Oppenheim and Putnam, 1958). This is just as true of those psychological theorists who resisted, or compromised with, the essential themes of so-called positivism (McDougall and Tolman, for instance) as it is of those who quite openly championed its most severe constraints (for instance, Hull and Skinner). And it is true despite the fact that both Carnap and the principal critic of positivism, Karl Popper, fully appreciated the distortion of Carnap's early advocacy of the unity thesis: Carnap, by being inexorably and reluctantly drawn, against his own persuasion, in Quine's direction (without actually advocating Quine's extreme charges); Popper, by doggedly shaping the principal alternative to the positivist conception of science, spiritually but uneasily still within the unity movement (without ever quite managing to articulate the structure of psychology or the human sciences or the relation between what Popper calls 'World 3' and the order of physical nature (see Popper, 1956/1982)).

The result is that when we think of psychology as a science, we are inevitably attracted to themes very much like Carnap's: so much so that to the extent that we find it difficult to accommodate the special features of psychology thus, we are more inclined to weaken psychology's claim to be a science than to consider seriously revising our picture of what a science is. In this regard, it is not negligible to remind ourselves that Freud's famous *Scientific Project* was, through the direction of his friend and early mentor, Wilhelm Fliess (and others), directly influenced by Helmholtzian and similar conceptions of science, that were the direct and continuous forerunners of the positivism of the Vienna Circle; also, that, by an instructive coincidence of history, the physiopsychologies of such theorists as Pavlov, Watson, and Thorndike converged at a very early and opportune time to lend additional authority to the vision that is most conveniently focused in Carnap's formulation. In fact, a very large part of more recent and contemporary conceptions of psychology, which, though they have surely superceded the classic forms of behaviorism and the various forms of reductive materialism (see Margolis, 1984a), have distinctly sought to reconcile their own novel directions with an adjusted view of what the unity of science program might legitimate.

All that is changing now – or is at least strenuously challenged – to the extent that the salient phenomena of psychology threaten to be recalcitrant one way or another to the regimentation of something like Carnap's vision; and to the extent that we are no longer completely persuaded that that vision or only models of science more or less congruent with its bent may be said to capture the essential features of a science. So the equilibration mentioned between theory and practice, is now all but impossible to resist. It will serve us, then, to summarize Carnap's early account of psychology and to identify what, regarding the field of psychology, is likely to place the greatest obstacles in the way of a smooth recovery of something like the unity of science model.

Aspects of the unity of science

Carnap's thesis (Carnap, 1932–33/1959) can hardly be more straightforwardly summarized than in his own words: '*physical language is a universal language*, that is, a language into which every sentence may be translated.' This is a version of a doctrine that Carnap himself calls *physicalism*. It was enunciated with the specific intent of affirming that '*Every sentence of psychology may be formulated in physical language*', which Carnap construed as a sub-thesis of the general claim. It is the most sweeping version but it is no more than a generic version of the theme of the *unity of science program*; and it was specifically interpreted by Carnap as promising detailed benefits of roughly three kinds.

First of all, it anticipated that the analysis of the highest-level theoretical statements (those for instance, as in theoretical physics, that appear to refer to and to characterize unobservable entities and processes, or, as in psychology, that appear to postulate unobservable internal mental states) may all, without exception, be effectively translated in the terms of an observational or empirical 'physical language'. In particular, this program was expected to offer a suitable analysis of physical laws or, more generally, of the logical or syntactical properties of laws or nomic universals, regardless of the field in which such regularities were taken to obtain.

These undertakings are breathtakingly comprehensive; but it is now entirely fair to say that, in spite of Carnap's indefatigable efforts, there is no satisfactory analysis (or 'reduction') of either statements about unobservable or theoretical entities and processes, or about physical or natural laws (which are known to generate puzzles about universal scope, the absence of reference to particular features or conditions of particular parts of the universe, and counterfactuality – that is, unobservable contrary-to-fact conditions affecting universality). There is not even a reasonable sense at the present time that, with continued effort, the required reduction can be gained. On the contrary, those attracted to a Carnapian-like vision are much more inclined nowadays to treat theoretical statements as false or fictional or instrumental or heuristic, and theoretical laws or laws in general as inference-tickets, promissory notes, inherently unconfirmable hypotheses, by which to guide actual empirical inquiry (see, for instance Cartwright, 1983; Popper, 1983; van Fraassen, 1980). One readily sees, therefore, the plain sense in which the theory of what a science is, or of what we may reasonably expect a science to accomplish, is bound to affect substantively the direction and governing convictions of research in empirical psychology.

In any case, the first sort of benefit concerns systematically linking the science of psychology with the entire family of sciences in terms of one or another version of the unity of science program. There are many technical variations of this program. But generally speaking, they all have to do with alternative options regarding simplicity, once something very much like Carnap's generic characterization of physicalism is adopted. Thus, for instance, it may or may not be the case that the descriptive predicates of the biological sciences are translatable, paraphrasable, or replaceable (by one strategy or another) by the descriptive predicates of basic physics; on the unity thesis, the descriptive vocabulary of biology will have to be (in some defensible sense) physical or physicalist – and the phenemona characterized by its use will have to be (in various possible ways) linked in lawlike respects to the phenomena of basic physics. Similarly, it may or may not be the case that the laws of 'emergent' domains like biology and psychology are subsumable under or derivable from (by one strategy or another) the laws of basic physics; but, on the unity thesis, the logical relationship between the laws of such domains and those of physics will have to be linked in ways congruent with the relationship between their respective vocabularies.

It is easy to see that there may be many variant forms of the unity thesis and, correspondingly, many variant views about what a physical language may be supposed to be, and how strictly questions of translation, paraphrase, equivalence, replacement, or elimination (of terms) should be treated. For example, Noam Chomsky (1980), construing language acquisition and linguisitic aptitude largely in biological terms – hence, construing the psychology of linguistic behavior largely in biological terms – specifically recommends enlarging the very notion of physical properties so that the science of linguistics may fairly be regarded as another physical science. It would not be unfair to say that, arguing in this manner, Chomsky shows the way to an imaginative, even free-wheeling, strategy for extending a version of the unity of science program where it is known to generate conceptual difficulties. In general, all the human sciences or studies or disciplines – hence, psychology, preeminently – strain the credibility of the unity thesis.

Carnap supposed that his project would afford a second sort of benefit centred on the advantages of *empiricism*, that is, a benefit regarding the nature and conditions of human cognitive competence (as scientists) and, in particular, the advantages of holding as strictly as possible to construing whatever might confirm a science as *empirically* responsible (cognitively responsible) solely in terms of an up-to-date version of the theory that all pertinent knowledge is fundamentally grounded in and systematically linked to our capacities for sensory perception (*empiricism*). Historically, this tendency in the philosophy of science is quite clearly associated with the conceptual orientation of the great eighteenth-century Scottish philosopher, David Hume (though not with the details of his own views, given the understanding of his time regarding the nature of the physical sciences themselves). That influence proceeds in a more-or-less continuous line, through John Stuart Mill (within the Anglo-American tradition) and Ernst Mach and Hermann von Helmholtz (within the Continental) – to mention the most salient figures of the refined empiricism of nineteenth-century theories of science. That empiricism reaches its various distinctive forms, in the twentieth century, both in the alternative positivisms of Schlick and Carnap and in Quine's devastating critique of the dual dogmas of empiricism (all the while, let it be said, Quine himself favors strategies very close in spirit to the empiricism he effectively unseats).

Quine dismantles two distinct 'dogmas', which he maintains are parts of one and the same error; and he himself recommends 'empiricism without the dogmas'. One dogma we have already mentioned: that there is a principled distinction between truths that are 'analytic', that depend on meanings independently of fact, and truths that are 'synthetic', that are grounded in matters of fact. The other dogma Quine calls *reductionism*, that is, 'the belief that each meaningful statement is equivalent to some logical construct upon terms which refer to immediate experience'. Carnap embraces both dogmas; and it is rea-sonably clear that Carnap's physicalism is the paradigm form of what Quine terms reductionism – and then undermines. Quine's point is, in part, that there is no way to maintain these distinctions except against the backdrop of the entire conceptual network and experience that shapes our very ability to pursue our inquiries (but not in any way in which the structure of that backdrop is itself straightforwardly testable – without an ulterior backdrop – empirically or in empiricist terms). We are forever caught within a working net of concept and experience, and there is no exit from it. Quine's object, here, is *not* against the physicalist program Carnap favors, but rather against the presumption that pursuing such a program can be vindicated, proposition by separate proposition (in a determinately individualized way), rather than against the backdrop of an 'entire' science – that is, on the condition, and only on the condition, of taking the entire body of science 'collectively', in the empiricist spirit (what has come to be called scientific *holism*). Quine's attitude here may very plausibly be taken to mark the most fashionable philosophical stance of much of recent analytic philosophy of science: Press on with physicalism and every allied program, but reject the need to vindicate any in terms of a thorough empiricism, a theory of meaning, a methodology or a cognitive account of the relationship between inquiry and the real world. The resultant venture has come to be called *pragmatism* – at least in certain quarters (see Rorty, 1979) – and represents a new attempt to prise a promising science away from a burdening philosophy. Ironically, although his own work encourages the tendency, Quine is in principle utterly opposed to the disjunction. There are in fact two 'pragmatisms' at work here: the holism of science and philosophy, and the rejection of all demands for the legitimation of science.

The empiricism of the Vienna Circle was confronted at a very early point in its career by the perceptive criticism of one of its own members, Otto Neurath (1932–33/1959), namely, that it is impossible to construe the would-be empiricist function of what Carnap called 'protocol sentences' as successfully capturing 'immediate experience' (in Quine's terms) or as providing any cognitive privilege or foundation for science (as both Carnap and Schlick wished and needed to claim) or even as being logically or epistemically distinct from any other ordinary empirical statements that would not have been advanced by Carnap as protocol sentences. The point is that the entire program of the unity of science, both explicitly as far as the early Carnap was concerned and to a large extent implicitly, rested on a theory of empirical knowledge that was seriously vulnerable to criticisms (advanced by Neurath and Quine) that, once taken seriously, raise systematic doubts about how to legitimate the unique or favored treatment accorded the physicalism that it depends upon. Carnap gradually attenuated his adherence to both the strong translation thesis and the privileged empiricism, though he never abandoned them altogether. The fortunes of the subsequent unity of science programs have, accordingly, had to be attenuated as well. In particular, it was crucial for Carnap's notion of empiricism that sentences reporting immediate experience be taken to be translatable into physicalist terms. Since, on the argument, this is now regarded as untenable, psychology suddenly becomes burdened by a series of admissions that countenance the inescapability of relying, for the sake of scientific rigor and responsibility, on introspective reports *and* on the conceptual impossibility of replacing such reports, one by one, by physicalist reductions. It would not be too extreme a judgment to hold that B. F. Skinner (1964), for example, consistently construes 'empirical' science (or psychology) in a way that strongly favors an empiricist temperament – somewhat closer to Carnap than to Quine – and that oscillates somewhere between paraphrasing introspective reports in behavioral terms and eliminating introspective reports altogether (without, however, quite explaining the cognitive standing of empirical investigation itself). In short, the viability of an extreme behaviorism of Skinner's sort depends not merely on replacing the study of introspective states with the study of observable behavior, but also on explaining the sense in which an observing scientist may be said actually to observe what he observes. So once again the fortunes of psychology as an empirical science are seen to be quite inseparable from whatever progress we can claim to make regarding the formulation of an adequate philosophy of science.

The third – in a way, the most powerful – benefit Carnap presumed his model would provide concerns what has come to be called *extensionalism*, or the extensionality thesis. One cannot say that it is a secret doctrine. Certainly, a very great part of twentieth-century psychology – also, allied disciplines, for example the so-called cognitive and informational sciences, as well as linguistics – is explicitly committed to one or another project falling within the scope of extensionalism. But it is curious nevertheless that many who work (in a somewhat narrow sense) in the empirical sciences are almost completely unfamiliar with the undertaking thus labeled. Hence, although in effect they may subscribe to it, they may not entirely grasp the immense attraction of the doctrine. It surely promises what, if it could be sustained, would be the most simple, the most unified, the most comprehensive vision of the whole of reality and of our knowledge of reality that we could ever hope to work out. It is only by explicating extensionalism, then, that one can fully appreciate the remarkably central role of the Vienna Circle's views and those of the unity of science program in shaping the scientific imagination of our own day.

One needn't hold that Carnap's influence was global. It wasn't. Or, that there are not very important currents in contemporary science and the theory of science opposed to the positivist and unity doctrines. There are, but it is certainly true that much of the resistance to positivism, on technical grounds (for instance, in terms of its failed theory of meaning), pretty well subscribes to extensionalism despite such demurrers. Similarly, quarrels within the unity camp have been every bit as vigorous as (in fact, more vigorous than) opposition to the movement itself. On purely historical grounds, we may fairly claim that the principal movements of empirical psychology and of theories of the science of psychology – right up to our own time – have been decidedly focused in terms of extensionalism, as well as in terms of quite parochial doctrines thought (whether rightly or wrongly) to be favored by extensionalism. The principal reason for pressing the point, apart from its intrinsic merit, is simply that we are thereby helped to appreciate the relatively homogeneous – or at least the distinctly convergent – conceptual cast of more than a century of psychology (and philosophy of psychology) toward the views that have most recently prevailed. On integrating such a picture of what the science of psychology has generally been thought to be, we prepare ourselves for entertaining all sorts of conceptual and programmatic difficulties that belong, on any reasonable view, within the precincts of psychology. In short, we are featuring Carnap primarily in a dialectical way; and we are sketching the conditions on which we may responsibly advocate a shift in orientation within empirical psychology and with respect to which, considering psychlogy to be a bona fide science, we may find ourselves obliged to concede ground regarding what constitutes the very structure of a science. So again we cannot fail to be struck by the symbiosis between what we do in psychology and what we theorize is legitimately open to attempt to do, *qua* science.

Turning to extensionalism itself, we may say that the doctrine has, when applied to empirical science, two distinct aspects. One holds, rather along the lines alrady cited from Carnap, that 'physical language is a universal language' – the universal language of science – where, in saying that, we affirm that physical language behaves 'extensionally'. The other explicates, in syntactic or logical terms, what the structure of any language must be if it is to behave 'extensionally'. Now, the first part of the thesis is often not as sanguinely conceived as Carnap conceived it. Not only is strict translation no longer thought required, or even thought possible; the extensionalist claim is usually treated as no more (and no less) than the ideal outcome of empirical inquiry – that hardly needs to begin with an effective translation program (or a program of looser paraphrase, or equivalence of replacement sentences in terms of truth values, or more informal substitutions of idiom without a close fit of truth values, or downright elimination of 'psychological' discourse). It is often said to be impossible in real-time terms, in effect in terms of the mortality of the race, to achieve the required translation or paraphrase, though we are assured (on what grounds, may be reasonably queried) that the substitution program is viable 'in principle'. So we have come a long way from the almost unguarded candor and enthusiasm of Carnap.

Carnap's basic claim still guides a good deal of contemporary psychology and the philosophy of such psychology, without needing to be given a complete vindication by way of anything like a proof; and whether the sketches of this supposed adequacy are genuinely compelling remains a serious point of contention. In any event, among philosophers, neither Carnap nor Quine nor any of their followers has as yet provided a knockdown or really forceful demonstration of how one should proceed to effectuate the extensionalist program; and, among psychologists, neither Hull nor Skinner nor any other well-known professional has as yet supplied a reasonably full sketch of how he would proceed extensionally (see Skinner, 1953, 1957; Tolman, 1978).

This is a quarrelsome claim, it must be said. It cannot be claimed that no significant efforts have ever been made to provide extensionalist replacements of the required sort. Many such efforts have been made. But all known sketches of replacement face two distinct difficulties. One – Skinner is perhaps the best-known victim of the charge (see Chomsky, 1959) – holds that the would-be substitution of idiom either smuggles into the analysis terms of just the sort that are to be replaced (for instance, introspective states or conditions of behavior that are meaningless or inoperative without the admission of such states) or arbitrarily eliminates such terms (and what they designate) without due argument (here, perhaps, Watson is the notorious culprit – see Watson, 1913/1963, 1925). The other difficulty – and, here, Quine is certainly the usual target (see Quine, 1960) – holds that the would-be substitutions cannot be justified on purely formal or syntactic grounds, although they may be explained in such terms and although they do have the installing of that sort of uniform logical structure as their avowed purpose. They must, on the argument, be justified in *empirical* terms, that is, in terms that have to do with pertinently interpreting or assigning meaning to the sentences in question, *in* the context of genuine scientific research.

Clearly, therefore, the meaning of 'empirical' bears in an essential way

cannot, in any sense in which the would-be replacements are to be taken
as part of the bona fide empirical work of the science of psychology, be
construed in terms of classical empiricist theories. The reason this is
important is just because the enlargement of the meaning of 'empirical' –
accommodating the would-be replacements in question – appears to
introduce in a central way just the sort of considerations regarding
psychological intentions, interpretations of meaning and the like, that call
into question our ability (in any principled sense one may reasonably
recommend) *to* construe psychological terms and phenomena along
extensionalist lines. In a word, the very activities of scientists constitute a
significant part of the phenomena a fully formed science of psychology
should be able to describe and explain; and it is in the setting of just
those activities – and of what, in a cognate way, obtains among other
psychological phenomena – that one is likely to generate salient
difficulties for the extensionalist program. At any rate, the issue risks
being obscured by entertaining that program in merely formal, not fully
empirical, terms. Alternatively put, the empirical pertinence of a syntactic
analysis of the language of psychology depends on the empirical use,
within the practices of the science, that that language is made to serve.
(We shall collect some benefits, later, from being careful here.)

The general assumption of physicalism (part of the very reason Carnap
champions the doctrine) is that it behaves extensionally. This has never
been completely demonstrated, for a number of reasons (that have
already been adumbrated). It is certainly not clear, even in the context of
physics, that high-level theoretical statements can be satisfactorily
analyzed, without remainder, in empirical terms – on any of various
alternative views of what 'empirical' means, suited to the practice of the
science; or that they can be provided with an analysis that
compartmentalizes their empirical content and whatever else encumbers
them for heuristic, explanatory, systematic or similar reasons. Secondly,
it is not clear at the present time that there is any satisfactory extensional
reading of physical laws, of universal claims that entail counterfactuals,
or of any demarcation of phenomenological and theoretical laws that
would vindicate a strong empirical bent of the required sort, congruent
with the general features of empirical physics. Finally it is not in the least
clear that the reasoning of inquiring scientists and their efforts at
explaining the phenomena they examine can be extensionally reduced. It
would not be responsive to dismiss the latter as irrelevant to the question,
since physics is a human science, even if its field does not countenance
the human as such; and since explanation is a genuine psychological
activity, not merely a formal instrument or canon of some sort.

Be these things as they may, the second aspect of extensionalism introduces technical considerations that we can only afford to sketch in the briefest way; they need not really occupy us in terms of a sustained account of the formal machinery usually called into play. Roughly speaking, in at least the interval between the pioneer work of Gottlob Frege and Bertrand Russell, various notions of an idealized logical syntax that could be fitted to the sentences of natural languages or portions of them (those, particularly, used in the most disciplined sciences) have been thought to exhibit certain characteristic properties. The sentences thus viewed are said to be simple or atomic, that is, not composed of other sentences or of incomplete parts of sentences marked as such, to which the bipolar truth values, true and false, may be assigned. All other well-formed sentences are said to be compound or complex constructions from such elements, in such a way that their own truth values, the same bipolar values, are assigned solely on the basis of the values assigned to atomic sentences and the use of certain so-called truth-functional connectives ('and', 'either . . . or', or the like) or operators of various kinds (so-called existential and universal quantifiers, or alethic and deontic operators or the like), where formulable rules indicate precisely how, on syntactic grounds alone and without exception, those values are to be determined. The rules of operation invoked are taken to be reasonable (or correct) idealizations (or abstractions) of the rules of deductive argument. Also, insofar as logic is viewed as an empirical discipline, the question arises whether and to what extent the portions of human language in actual use can be shown to exhibit (or to justify being replaced by an idiom exhibiting) the required extensionality.

Carnap, then, was the beneficiary of the refinement of just such a logical canon, brought to a level of high achievement in the early part of our century, more or less at the same time as the pioneer achievements of relativity and quantum physics. In empirical psychology, increasingly within our own time, at least in the Anglo-American tradition, one cannot deny that the formal extensionalist program has been very powerfully championed – in a way that is more and more remotely connected with the active pursuit of a full unity-of-science venture, that would specifically link psychology and physics. It is in fact in the work of Donald Davidson (1970), very closely associated with Quine's work, that one perhaps finds the most fashionable sketch (it is and can be only a sketch) of the full intent of the physicalism, unity of science, and extensionalism that characterizes the most subtle versions of these doctrines to date – specifically intended to be applied to the psychological and social sciences. There is a general convergence with

Davidson's vision, to be noted in current cognitive and informational sciences and in the theory of behavior and linguistics, even where Davidson himself cannot be supposed to have been directly influential in shaping the various pictures of the disciplines involved. But it is quite instructive about the current state of the philosophy of psychology to take note of the fact that Davidson himself relies very heavily on the formal semantics of the well-known Polish logician, Alfred Tarski (see 1956/1983; 1944, for a more informal account of his theories), who has pursued the best-known program for an extensionalized account of truth that might be suited to natural languages – but who expressly declared himself convinced that the canon could not be applied to natural languages either in general or without significant distortion. Davidson obviously does not accept Tarski's constraint, though he has yet to demonstrate how to escape the pitfalls Tarski believed unavoidable.

Obstacles to a scientific psychology

We need, now, to reflect on two options. The theory of science we have just sketched may be taken (as it is by many) to be the 'true' theory or a fair approximation to same; or it may be taken to be a convenient, though skewed, idealization against the backdrop of which the actual science of psychology (undoubtedly, other sciences as well) may be perspicuously characterized by way of contrast. The Carnap-to-Davidson route prefers the first; and, quite frankly, we shall here prefer the second. But in so saying, it would not go amiss to mention that *wherever* piecemeal achievements in accord with the first view can be genuinely vindicated, such achievements need never be denied by protagonists of the second sort. The latter need only maintain that, in particularly central or important ranges of the domain of psychology, the first sort of program either does not work, does not seem promising, seems to depend on a mere *obiter dictum* in the face of strenuous difficulties, ignores salient puzzles, postpones essential confrontations or the like. There seems to be no way of demonstrating once and for all that programs of the first sort could not possibly succeed. So seen, the evidence suggests that the assessment of competing programs for empirical psychology – and for their philosophical complements – must be handled in a relatively informal way. But that need not lead us into thinking that reasonably strong conclusions cannot be drawn regarding the compared merits of the opposing views.

This brings us then to the promised obstacles in the way of a smooth unity of science program.

Favoring economy, we may say that the science of psychology is first and primarily the science of human psychology. This is not to deny of course that animal psychology is of the greatest importance or that a great many of the most influential experimental psychologists have actually preferred to study sub-human animals – *and* to risk generalizing or inferring from the one to the other. But this seemingly innocuous difference in investigative taste may well distract us from a more decisive consideration. For it is impossible, in examining human psychology, to ignore the central role of cognition or cognitive states: knowing, believing, reasoning, thinking, intending, fearing, perceiving, feeling and the like; and if, particularly among the primates and the vertebrates, cognitively pertinent states are conceded, the question cannot fail to arise about their appropriate conceptual analysis. The very investigative efforts of human scientists, reflectively applied or otherwise, would make it preposterous to attempt to construct a psychology that did not reconcile the analysis of cognitive states with its larger philosophical orientation – for instance, with a version of the unity of science program. And, on any known theory of cognitive states, there is generally now conceded to be no way of avoiding admitting, at least initially, so-called *intentional* states, states that exhibit a certain internal 'aboutness' or 'directedness', states that (on a heuristically perspicuous model, if not on more realistic grounds) must be characterized in propositional terms.

To put the point flatly, it makes no sense to say that Tom *has a belief* (believes something or other) without being prepared to add that what Tom believes is a 'proposition' (or is perspicuously rendered or designated by a sentence or the like) – that Tom believes *that* . . . , even if we are unable to supply the required proposition or if there is no one such formulation that could reasonably be expected to fix what Tom believes or even if we are not at all sure or clear about what 'in the mind' could possibly answer to what we mean to designate in supplying the proposition in question. This single peculiarity, so essential to and so distinctive of human psychology, is, it must be said, characteristically given scant attention in most of the experimental orientations influenced by the unity model.

We are suddenly plunged, by this single consideration, into a cluster of difficulties that, on any plausible view, cannot be ignored *if* psychology is to be the science of pertinent aspects of the human condition. Contrary to what Carnap enthusiastically affirmed, there is no known way by which to reduce the analysis of cognitive states to physical states; without such a reduction, the prospects of a *theory* of science inclining toward the unity model – as distinct from the prospects of an advanced psychology – must seem seriously threatened indeed. Furthermore, if cognitive states are conceded sub-human animals and prelinguistic infants (as, clearly, the studies of such investigators as Köhler, Lorenz, von Frisch, Gibson, Piaget, Premack, Griffin and others oblige us to consider – even if we remain skeptical or ambivalent or attempt to avoid actually admitting the propositional model as any more than heuristic, when applied to lower animals at least), then *animal psychology is to that extent conceptually parasitic on human psychology.*

Broadly speaking, there have been three strategies of reduction for the proper disciplining of cognitive states *vis-à-vis* the fortunes of something like the unity model. One strategy flatly ignores the complications of what we have just identified as the 'intentional' nature of cognitive states. Carnap's translational approach is now generally conceded to be naive and unworkable, since, on any familiar view, the intentional and physicalistic idioms are not intertranslatable – even if it is true that the 'mental' states putatively described as intentional are actually entirely physical. So, one strategy holds that, one way or another, the mental (or psychological: not necessarily equivalent notions) just *is* the physical; hence, the complexities of the intentional may be safely ignored. But, as in such well-known philosophical discussions of the issues as those of Smart (1959/1962) and Davidson (1970), the required demonstration is noticeably lacking. This would not, perhaps, be a decisive difficulty *if* it could be shown that a suitable physicalist, behaviorist, functionalist or similar approach to the normal range of psychological phenomena (see Margolis, 1984a) could be counted on to facilitate a reasonably adequate, reasonably powerful run of descriptions, predictions and explanations for the thus-adjusted psychology. Unfortunately, at the present time, there is no such psychology. Moreover, much of the dispute about that failing tends to center on what should be taken to be the import of such phrases as, 'at the present time': does this suggest that we may expect to make significant progress in the foreseeable future, or is it merely a piece of tact advising us that we have made a wrong turn? In any case, the first strategy is no strategy at all: it is only a promissory note.

That promise has been pursued along two principal lines – if we may oversimplify for the sake of an inessential convenience. Either the reduction of cognitively pertinent phenomena has been conducted in 'peripheral' terms, that is, in terms of observable behavior and the like (where 'behavior' is conceded a certain elastic sense, not necessarily confining us to the full-fledged actions, activity, behavior of 'molar' organisms alone, or where behavior may be supplemented by attention to physiological or biochemical changes thought to be adjunctive to it, but without attention to putative 'central states' or 'central mental states'); or the reduction has been conducted in 'central state' terms with or without attention to behavioral, dispositional or similar considerations of the 'peripheral' sort. The constraining notion here is that central states (including but not necessarily restricted to cognitive states) cannot, in principle, be reduced to peripheral behavior. For example, variable but incompletely enumerated dispositions to behave are bound to satisfy variable truth conditions and could not, empirically, singly or collectively, determine the truth conditions on which given central states would obtain. The issue is a subtle but decisive one, marking a fatal logical weakness in Skinner's sort of behaviorism (see Nelson, 1982; or the more accessible Nelson, 1969). For it signifies, among other things, that one could not even formulate in behaviorist terms the thesis that humans and animals are automata – whether or not that thesis were true. Consequently, it would be impossible to describe satisfactorily machine stimulations of human intelligence, in behaviorist terms.

Taken as developed programs, Skinner (1953) may well provide the clearest exemplar of the first line of argument; and the Australian philosopher, D. M. Armstrong (1968, 1973) may well have provided the clearest exemplar of the second. Both are strongly drawn to something like the unity model; and yet both, on reasonable (though also disputable) grounds, may be said to introduce, in the very analysis of the 'intentional', ulterior intentional factors that threaten to be ineliminable or that (as in Skinner's work) simply fail to recognize the actual intentional complexity of the phenomena they themselves admit. (We are here, of course, interested in merely presenting the principal disputes and strategies.) The 'peripheralist' (the term is only a term of art) tends to ignore the intentional complexity of cognitive states, since he does not admit central states. This is surely the most characteristic feature of Skinner's lifelong undertaking, and marks him much more distinctively than do his objections to confusing biology with psychology. This bears directly on his own misgivings about Watson, Pavlov, and Hull, as well as on the criticism, implied or explicit, of his own views, as in the ingenious work of the ethologist, Tinbergen, who, at least at the level of the lower animals, might reasonably be said to have favored a moderate form of behaviorism (without, however, ever dismissing central states) or as in the equally ingenious work of the ecologically-minded J. J. Gibson (who similarly attempted to reconcile behavioral and central-state considerations). Both Tinbergen and Gibson attempt, in rather different ways, to acknowledge the role of central states governing behavior, while avoiding the admission of cognitive states (in Tinbergen, through instinctual mechanisms; in Gibson, through the preestablished harmonies of ecological niches).

In a fair sense, the problem of cognition serves as a pivot for the recent turn in empirical psychology and the related so-called cognitive sciences in coming to favor versions of *functionalism* (see Block, 1980, vol. 1; Dreyfus, 1972/1979) or of even bolder *nativisms* (associated most recently with the theories of Chomsky and his younger associate, Fodor (1975)), or in the distinct revival of interest in the views of Piaget and of his important Russian critic, Lev Vygotsky (1934/1962, 1978).

But in acknowledging the peculiar persistence of its conceptual puzzles, we would do well to remind ourselves that the intentional idiom, mentioned earlier, was largely prepared, for modern readers and theorists at least, by the nineteenth-century German philosopher, Franz Brentano, who first, effectively, recovered the medieval conception of 'intentionality' for use in the context of empirical psychology (1874/1973); and that Brentano's notion was contested and adjusted in a powerful way by his greatest and most influential student, Edmund Husserl, the founder of phenomenology. Certainly, through Husserl (see Merleau-Ponty, 1942/1963), through Christian Ehrenfels (Brentano's student and the founder of gestalt psychology), through Alexius Meinong (another of Brentano's students, who established the first experimental psychology laboratory in Austria) and more diffusely and more indirectly (converging to some extent with Husserl) through Freud and through the great German experimentalist, Wilhelm Wundt, intentional if not phenomenological analysis began to gather force in empirical psychology and in the philosophy of psychology in a way that may be reasonably construed as shaping an alternative conception of science (and psychology) opposed to the model favored by the unity of science movement.

In this regard, it is perhaps not unhelpful to note that Wundt, whose pioneer experimental physiological psychology was decidedly influenced by the Helmholtzian vision, was also clearly influenced by Husserl, particularly in terms of admitting large societal and historical forces preforming and affecting individual consciousness. To what extent the opposing currents of the unity model and of a broadly conceived phenomenology can be reconciled is bound to become an increasingly strategic issue in the eclectic milieu of contemporary Western psychology and philosophy. Or, broadening our picture and muting doctrinal quarrels, the question of reconciling the distinct discipline of the unity model and the dawning appreciation of the role of cognitive, societal and historical influences upon individual psychology (which, in a way, indifferently collects phenomenological, Marxist, Freudian, Piagetian, structuralist, hermeneutic, semiotic and even more loosely defined themes) can hardly fail to be featured in the next generation of empirical psychology and the philosophy of psychology.

The theme of intentionality has a double function. For one thing, it permits a perspicuous first approach (at least) to the complexities of cognitive states – in effect, to what is most ineliminable and most salient in human psychology. For our purposes, it hardly matters whether specific versions of the idiom of intentional analysis are treated heuristically or in a deeper realist sense: the designated phenomena are quite real, and it is their puzzling (and actual) features that the intentional idiom is supposed to display. The most prominent distinction of intentional phenomena is generally admitted to concern their 'aboutness', that is, that mental states, cognitively qualified states, appear to be peculiarly complex despite being best represented as monadic – as designated by monadic predicates. An intentional state – believing that Cairo is the capital of Egypt, fearing an earthquake, searching for a cufflink – is designated by a predicate whose complexity, at least with respect to whether its syntactic structure is monadic or polyadic, is not affected by however we choose to represent the structure of its (indissoluble) 'internal object' (or 'internal accusative'). Such predicates are incomplete in a peculiar way if no reference is made to their 'sense', what the states they designate are 'about' or 'directed to'. This is true even of the famous predicate, 'anxious', since there may be no specific 'object' that one is anxious about (neurotic anxiety); but, as is often said, the absence of a specific object is the principal clue to the very 'aboutness' of neurotic anxiety.

The second function of the theme of intentionality specifically concerns a direct challenge to the doctrine of extensionalism. For it was characteristically claimed in its name – it was so claimed by Brentano (though in certain questionable ways) – that intensionality (that is, non-extensionality) was a mark of intentionality (aboutness). Apart from Brentano's arguments, it is certainly true that the champions of extensionality – Carnap, Quine and Davidson at least – supposed that the vindication of physicalism would eliminate the puzzles of intensionality *by* eliminating or neutralizing intentionality. In fact, it is one of the boldest, most radical speculations of the extensionalists that the ascription of mental states and their intensional complexities is essentially the result of indissolubly locking the intensional features of language into the structure of intentional (and related) predicates – and that that can be avoided in principle. The claim has as yet not been demonstrated to the satisfaction of its opponents. There you have the clue to the great contest, at the level of both empirical psychology and the philosophy of psychology, between the unity model and those models that, one way or another, mean to recover the complexity of cognitive states. It must be said at once, however, that the admission of cognitive states is not tantamount to the defeat of extensionalism: this is just the point of Davidson's generalized application of Tarski's formal account of truth to the empirical domains of psychology and the social sciences. But there can be little doubt that it is and will remain one of the most nagging problems confronting what may reasonably be posited as an adequate account of what a science is (admitting psychology) and of what manner of inquiry empirical psychology can and should pursue (conceding the incompletely resolved puzzles of intentionality).

The truth is that the question of intentionality (and the puzzles of its intensional complexity) is not and cannot be restricted to the question of the logic of so-called intentional predicates. For one thing, the question arises within the range of narrowly linguistic instruments, with regard to other features and devices of language – for instance, with regard to reference, meaning, quotation, indirect discourse. And for another, language cannot itself be regarded as a merely formal instrument, the analysis or revision of which can be convincingly undertaken without regard to the actual behavior and practice of the apt speakers of natural languages. The essential point is that linguistic activity, linguistic ability and competence, linguistic dispositions, the very 'language' or lingual nature of human sensibility, thought, consciousness, behavior, desire and feeling, all point unmistakably to the *psychological reality* of language at the human level. Apart from the extremely marginal occurrence of so-called 'wild' children, there are no human societies that lack language, that fail to rear children in such a way that their normal development entails acquiring the mastery of a specific language and the formation of 'languaged' life.

Any psychology that is, in the primary sense already affirmed, a human psychology will have to come to terms with the social nature of the acquisition of such a language and its implications. It is here that the full import of the intentional thesis must be found – which, precisely for reasons pertinent to *cognitive* abilities, cannot be rightly restricted, in any empirically responsible way, to what are said to be entirely neutral, purely logical or syntactic analyses and adjustments.

This perhaps essentially explains the lively interest, in current psychology, in the doctrines of such diverse thinkers as the American pragmatist, George Herbert Mead (1934), the Ludwig Wittgenstein who replaces the stark extensionalism of the *Tractatus* by the suggestive notion (of the *Philosophical Investigations*) of contingent and variable 'forms of life', and the Marxian Vygotsky. The convergent interest in these and similar figures points to the increasing polarization, almost globally, between the two great movements we have been at pains to identify. It certainly deserves to be noted that the linguistic, societal, historicized complexities of human existence are, characteristically, either ignored, not featured, assigned a logically dependent role with respect to the primary tasks of psychology or regarded as hardly complicating or perhaps not even entirely pertinent to the discipline itself – in the views and inquiries of those most strongly committed to extensionalism, physicalism, and the unity of science model. The reverse is dramatically obvious in the work of those occupied with the puzzles of cognition and intentionality so central to the human condition, even among those familiar with and distinctly attracted to the rigor of the 'analytic' model (see, for instance, Harré, 1979, 1984).

Having said all this, we must come back to the obstacles we promised. Here, once again, economy is the best policy. There are really two profound conceptual puzzles that affect everything that can be said about whatever is distinctively human and that are, nevertheless, not at all satisfactorily understood at the present time. To mention them, therefore, is to set the agenda for the future of psychology and the philosophy of psychology – and much more of course. They force a promising confrontation between the champions of the large movements of psychological theory we have just been sketching, and they raise in an inescapable way the general question of whether and in what sense psychology may be said to be an autonomous science, a science genuinely separable in professional and operational terms from the entire array of social and human sciences. In reviewing these two puzzles, we must be ready for what may be entailed in segregating the psychology of individuals and so-called social psychology and in segregating psychologies from sociologies, anthropologies, histories and the like.

We should perhaps formulate our two puzzles in a way that features their puzzling nature:

1 Natural human languages and the capacity for acquiring and using them must have emerged from sub-human forms of life and even from pre-vital physical nature; and yet human language appears to be *sui generis*, not explicable in terms restricted to purely physical or sub-linguistic processes;

2   Only individual human beings are effective agents, whether acting singly or aggregatively; and yet whatever humans characteristically do, as in communicating linguistically and in acting in ways distinctive of their historical cultures – according to their institutions, traditions, rules and norms, and practices for instance – the structure of languages, institutions, traditions, rules and norms and the like appears not to be describable or explicable in terms restricted to the agency of mere individuals, however psychologically developed.

One must consider what would follow from embracing a strongly affirmative reading of these two theses: it would be an immediate consequence that the unity of science program was fatally flawed; that physicalism and extensionalism were false or impossible to vindicate at this level of debate; and that psychology could not, in principle, be regarded as an autonomous science. These extraordinarily sweeping consequences flow directly from two familiar claims, against which no one at the present time has a really good or compelling counterargument or strategy. *If* they could be shown to be incoherent claims, then of course all would be well with the doctrines affected. But they seem reasonably coherent – and, moreover, they may well be true. They also have the joint effect of substantially altering the context for examining intentionality. It is in fact an unorthodox suggestion, but one that our two theses effectively recommend, that intentionality is either primarily a feature of *societal* life, in that sense in which the social cannot in principle be reduced to the individual (even where aggregatively construed) or else it is a feature of a *symbiotic* conception of the psychological in which individual agency can be identified only in a societal milieu and in which the social obtains in actual or realist terms only as a characterizable feature of the agency of individuals. There may be a sense in which Husserl, particularly toward the end of his career (1954/1970), viewed the intentional in terms of social history; but the canonical view of intentionality, both with respect to Brentano and Husserl, is decidedly centered in the cognitive life of individuals. It is similarly so viewed, even where it is thought to be effectively disarmed, in the critical efforts of theorists like Quine and Davidson.

In the philosophical literature, the first of our two puzzles (1) has come to be called the problem of *emergence* (see Feigl, 1958/1967); the second (2), the problem of *methodological individualism* (see Popper, 1961). There is no prospect, given the general account already provided, of constructing a responsible psychology or an informed philosophy of psychology or of what, conceding psychology, it is to be a science, without passing through these two puzzles. To attempt to resolve them here would take us too far afield; the effort could not possibly be restricted to the fortunes of psychology. But we must provide at least a sketch of just what the bearing of these puzzles is on the pursuit of psychological inquiry and the status of psychology as a science.

Puzzle (1) suggests a fundamental difference between the natural and the human sciences. In general, the physical sciences have been more and more insistently focused, in historical terms, upon the discovery or postulation of *fundamental* entities, forms of energy, and lawlike processes by reference to which *everything* rightly falling within *physical nature* can be explained or perspicuously redescribed for purposes of explanation. It is easy to see that such an orientation is just the inspiration for the unity of science program. It needs to be said that 'emergent' phenomena and the laws governing such 'emergent' phenomena need not, consistently with all forms of the unity model, be strictly described or accountable solely in terms of the properties of whatever is posited as fundamental to physical nature: emergent phenomena and the laws of emergent phenomena may be linked, for descriptive and explanatory purposes, only with the properties and behavior of entire systems of phenomena said to be of a next-'lower' or next-more fundamental level of complexity than the level in question (see Bunge, 1977a, b). Such emergence will, then, be construed as compatible with a larger reductive venture, but will not be as radically conceived as, say, in Carnap's completely translational model. In particular, it will require a continuous conceptual, descriptive, and explanatory linkage through all the putatively more complex 'levels' of organization, from the most fundamental to the most complex. For instance, it may (but it need not) require that the phenomena of a given complex be entirely composed of the elements of next-lower level of physical complexity – where, at each such level, the governing laws will not be directly derivable in a deductive way from the laws governing the next-lower level together with conditions obtaining at that level, simply because the elements of the higher level are describable only in terms of emergent relationships holding at that higher level. Emergent forces may appear as a result of such organization, that are not describable or explainable in terms sufficient for the elements not thus combined or related, at the next-lower level. Looser connections among different levels are also possible. It is in fact just this sort of thinking that is involved in distinguishing biology from physics, within the unity model (see Causey, 1977).

But *if* favoring (1), language cannot be thus described or explained, if there is a systematic logical discontinuity between explanations regarding physical nature and human existence or culture, then the very explanatory undertakings of psychology cannot conform with what we have just noted as characteristic of the physical sciences. *The human sciences – psychology, in particular – cannot be committed to the pursuit of fundamental phenomena and processes, in the sense of 'fundamental' suited to the physical sciences.* There you have the clue to the master contest of all contemporary philosophies of science. The issue is essentially 'empirical', in that relaxed sense already introduced – once we have satisfied ourselves that the alternative here raised is at least coherent. It will be seen to be coherent if something like the following considerations are conceded. First of all, *all* sciences, all descriptive and explanatory efforts, are the work of human agency, in the double sense of process and product. They are all, certainly, linguistically conducted and linguistically formulated achievements. As such, they partake of the same paradox as (1) itself: thus, there is no known physicalist description or explanation of human science – whether physics or psychology. And secondly, as in the physical sciences, the phenomena to be explained (the explananda) form the conclusion of an argument (whether hypothetico-deductive, as the unity people believe – see Hempel, 1965 – or not) and the premises of the argument (the explanans) will conform to the best achievements of the empirical sciences to date. But if that is so, then the mode of explanation in psychology and the other human sciences cannot, for formal reasons alone, be thought to be incoherent: the logical structure of the arguments involved need not be pertinently different, at any given stage of the work of a particular science, as between psychology and physics.

This of course does not yet make sense of the gap or discontinuity mentioned. But it does go some distance toward showing that its admission is not likely to risk incoherence – although it may well risk a general sense of disappointment in the world and in ourselves. But of course it need not do that either.

The point of the paradox may be put in the following way. *If* the phenomena at the human or cultural or linguistic level are emergently *sui generis*, so that they cannot be described or accounted for satisfactorily in terms of the vocabulary and laws of lower-level phenomena, together with new compositional or organizational complexities themselves conceptually linked to ways of combining the elements or emergent systems at lower levels, then there cannot be a descriptive and explanatory continuum *ascending* from the most fundamental to the most complex level of organization. That would signify a failure of the unity of science vision. But *if* description and explanation are themselves among the psychologically real phenomena that any pertinently competent science must address, *and if* they exhibit the emergent, *sui generis* properties in question, then it would not be unreasonable to attempt to explain that *emergence* (from lower-level biological and physical nature) by way of conjectures controlled by whatever causal or lawlike regularities were thought to obtain at any and all levels involved, including prominently the *sui generis* phenomena to be accounted for. In that sense, there may be a *descending* continuum of explanation – which, to be sure, would be logically and methodologically weaker than what, on the unity model, would be expected from an ascending continuum. Still, in the sense immortalized by Aristotle, we cannot expect more rigor than the domain permits; and it may well be that, in principle, there is no effective way of achieving the admittedly elegant order of an ascending continuum of description and explanation.

To put the point in human terms, it may well be that, given that humans *are* languaged and pursue science, they cannot inquire into anything in a way that is not indissolubly affected by their possessing their language and cognitive ability. Hence, every human science may be an *artifact* of that emergent level at which, reflectively, humans, thus structured, do pursue their inquiries. In short, the irony we may be facing is that science itself may be of such a nature that it must, as a psychologically and socially real phenomenon, baffle the unity of science vision.

There are many obvious analogues of this problem: for example, the Piagetian problem of genetic epistemology, of theorizing about the developmental stages of infantile intelligence – which can only be provided in the order of descent from a full-fledged level of human performance; or, the problem of comparing bee 'languages' with human language – which once again, can only be managed by conceptually depriving a full human language of graduated powers until we arrive at what we imagine insect intelligence to be (see Bennett, 1964); or, the problem, the crucial Kantian (or Kantian-like) problem, of determining discrepancies between the natural similarities and natural class-like clustering of phenomena and the culturally contingent categories of human construction–which, once again, can only be managed by comparing, at (and confined within) the level of human language, the classificatory schemes of different societies (see Rosch, 1973). We must remind ourselves, here, that our purpose is only to confirm the coherence and potential fruitfulness of the human sciences construed in accord with (1).

Puzzle (2) is also intimately linked with the analysis of language. Because there is no adequate theory of natural languages that does not address the complex uniformities and tolerance of variability that characterize a human language both diachronically and synchronically. The conventional view is that human language is governed by a finite set of formulable rules from finitely many elements that may be formed and transformed in admissible ways. This way of putting matters is distinctly formal and asocial, that is, posed utterly without regard to the dynamics of actual human societies. It is noteworthy, therefore, that the most developed conceptions of this sort, either as in structuralisms based on Saussure's distinction between *langue* and *parole* (see Hjeimslev, 1943/1961; Saussure, 1916/1959) or as in the various forms of nativism led by Chomsky's attempt to biologize language (see Chomsky, 1980; Fodor 1975), theorize that language is in some essential respect both a closed system and a system whose essential properties have nothing really to do with human sociality and history. Chomsky treats the 'deep grammar' of natural language in terms of species-specific genetic endowment; and he holds that languages are not really learned but essentially 'develop' like organ systems within the body. He believes that, in this regard, he is pursuing the inquiries of cognitive psychology. The trouble with Chomsky's view is, first, that it attempts to segregate the syntactic structure of natural language from the semantic, experiential, practical, historically shifting uses of language and it posits that syntactic structure as being of primary and fundamental importance to the entire range of the more superficial variabilities of human language; and, secondly, that it admits the syntactic element to be no more than a 'modular' ingredient in the interfunctioning competences that other 'modular' ingredients contribute (in vindicating our total picture of language), but has absolutely nothing to say about such other modules or how they may affect the single module Chomsky isolates. From an entirely different perspective, though with surprisingly similar results, Saussure admits that actual speech, the linguistic intercourse of human beings, has as such nothing to contribute to the science of language, which depends rather on a radical abstraction from the vagaries of contingent use.

Both lines of argument may be regarded as attempts to enlarge the scope of the unity of science model, in just those areas of inquiry in which the reductive impetus associated with physicalism (certainly in the Carnapian sense) has no real prospect of succeeding. There is, however, a very strong extensionalist bent that these efforts exhibit. Hence, it has proved entirely possible, as Fodor's recent popularity among those interested in psychological and linguistic studies (favoring a strong extensionalism) attests, to combine the nativism of Chomsky and the extensionalism of Davidson (see Fodor, 1975). This is, in fact, the characteristic American direction in which biology and linguistics tend to be linked in order to provide a picture of psychology redeeming the unity of science model in what is presumed to be an up-to-date way (see for instance Fodor, 1983). In effect, what Fodor recommends is that we assign a nativist supply of finitely many concepts to the genetics of the species that may be used in accord with correspondingly innate, finite rules of combination, and that (thus used) obey Davidson's exten-sionalized treatment of predicates (along Tarskian lines). This has the very odd result of disallowing the social learning of new concepts as well as of new ways of organizing and using concepts. It is clearly inspired by a will to resist the paradox of (1) and the introduction of a rich societal dimension (2) to human learning, human language, human conception, human cognition; it therefore serves quite neatly to clarify the point of the famous debate between Chomsky and Piaget (see Piattelli-Palmarini, 1980). For Piaget, as opposed to Chomsky (and Fodor), wished to preserve richer and more powerful forms of intelligent behavior, through learning, in spite of the fact that he also impoverishes (as Vygotsky saw at an early date) the social processes by which distinctly human behavior is shaped.

The upshot is that there is a contest gathering force, within the scope of psychology, regarding the social formation of distinctly human aptitudes and behavior – in that sense in which the *social* signifies at the very least the historical contingencies by which individual humans acquire and learn to use particular natural languages and to work within the institutionalized practices of their own societies. The analyses of these phenomena are noticeably difficult; but the principal intuition that guides inquiry regarding them, in accord with (2), is simply that *languages, traditions, social practices, institutions, rules and the like are, in some sense, 'possessed' by entire societies.* Generally speaking, theory must avoid, here, the hopeless fiction of actual collectivities functioning as psychologically apt agents (say, in the manner of Durkheim); it must, at the same time, avoid either radically biologized accounts or accounts that treat the attributes of societies (affecting individual agency, as in speech) as analyzable in a reductive way, in terms of attributes restricted to an individualistic psychology.

It is noteworthy that Karl Popper, who may well be the best-known advocate among philosophers of science (1950, 1961) of a strong methodological individualism, (allegedly pitted against Marxist and

Hegelian views), always insists (though without due explanation) upon the nonreducibility of societal and institutional predicates, with respect to the predicates of individualistic agency. There are, therefore, at least two forms of *methodological individualism* (the term has been popularized by Popper, if not actually coined by him): on the more extreme version, not only is agency assignable only to individual humans (taken singly or aggregatively), but the descriptive and explanatory terms used in characterizing human agency are always expressible in terms adequate to the description of biologically individual agents or of the actual relationships holding between such agents already first introduced. There is no promising evidence that the option is empirically reasonable. In the more moderate version (Popper's, though the fact is often not noticed), the actual agents are only individuals, but a background account of social institutions is both admissible and required for the complexities of language and culture, that cannot be reduced in the manner favored by the first version. Assuming the impossibility of giving a merely biological or psychologically individualistic account of any of the principal forms of individual behavior within human societies, one begins to understand why there should be emerging at the present time a distinct appreciation of the work of a number of seminal thinkers who have obviously grasped important aspects of the profoundly social nature of human existence and human aptitude and intelligence. Among these may be listed – but only listed – Mead, Wittgenstein, Husserl, Vygotsky; and, perhaps in more specialized ways, J. L. Austin (1962), Mikhail Bakhtin (1981), Michel Foucault (1966/1970), Pierre Bourdieu (1972/1977) and others who are not likely to be considered central to the development of professional psychology.

Top-down and bottom-up psychologies

The thread of our story is leading us inexorably to an essential contrast: that between *top-down* and *bottom-up* psychologies. Broadly speaking, the point of the contrast is that between psychologies that favor the ascending continuum of description and explanation so distinctive of the physical sciences and psychologies that favor a descending continuum, in the sense linked to the emergent, *sui generis* features of human language and culture. To focus the contrast thus facilitates classifying a great many alternative psychologies and helps to collect the salient features of the descending continuum, that threaten psychology with more and more heterodox considerations.

To anticipate: the upshot of our account, favoring top-down theories, would have it that the psychologies that have prevailed more or less to the present time and have been carefully honed in terms of the empiricism and positivism ranging from the period of Helmholtz and Mach and Mill to that of the Vienna Circle – both in the Continental and the Anglo-American traditions – are not likely to resemble those bound to flourish in the next generation of theories. This is not to say that psychologies very much like those already mentioned or sketched will not be generated in large numbers in the interval to come; or that the newer kinds of psychology we are prophesying will not attempt to reconcile themselves with the entirely admirable rigor and contributions of the other general movement. It is to say only that the spirit of the newer psychologies is definitely changing and that the achievements of the other, wherever incorporated, will inevitably have to be assigned a distinctly subordinate role to whatever is forcefully entailed by the opposition between top-down and botton-up strategies. There would otherwise be no point at all to insisting on that opposition.

Two preliminary observations must be made about the contrast between top-down and bottom-up strategies. Some believe that, ideally, the two should be equivalent or yield equivalent results or yield results that fall within the same orderly system of explanation – where the system is itself *bottom-up* (in a strong sense associated with the unity of science model or the ascending continuum of explanation). The optimism is open to serious dispute, but it is clear that its more-or-less symmetrical picture of the two strategies can only serve an ulterior asymmetry that ultimately denies the problematic status of what we have been calling the emergent and *sui generis* nature of language and its allied phenomena. The second consideration draws our attention to the important fact that, once the strategies are *not* thus construed, they will be seen to be of conceptually quite different sorts.

The bottom-up strategy may be said to be broadly *compositional*, in the sense that, either empirically or logically, inquiry pursues the basic elements or atoms of the entire domain to be examined, from which, progressively, we are to build more and more complex structures reaching at last to the complexities of human language and culture. (The term 'compositional' is intended here in an informal and partially metaphoric sense.) The top-down strategy is *factorial*, in the sense that, beginning with the highest or relatively high orders of complexity – in our present context, the empirical realities of language cognition, social existence, culture and the like – we attempt to formulate distinctions of a descriptive and explanatory sort, relationally introduced and justified by reference to the very complexities to be explained. (Unlike the structuralists, we need not regard such distinctions as designating mere relata – the possibility of linking up with some bottom-up strategy is always open).

The terminology itself ('top-down' and 'bottom-up') may be regarded as capturing alternatives that belong jointly to the history of the empirical sciences and to the current jargon of comparing artificial intelligence (AI) and human intelligence. The idiom has been popularized by many, notably by the American philosopher of psychology and enthusiast of AI simulation, Daniel Dennett (1978). Dennett advances the interesting claim that the bottom-up strategies of stimulus-response behaviorism and (what he calls) 'neuron signal physiological psychology' are both unproductive – the first because stimuli and responses appear not to be promising 'atoms', the second because even if neuronal impulses are promising, there are too many of them and they are too complexly involved in given phenomena to be useful as yet in a bottom-up science. Dennett also advances the claim that simulation is, in effect, a *top-down* strategy. Nevertheless, the fact remains that Dennett treats the two strategies symmetrically *and* means to introduce the AI model in a top-down manner in order, precisely, to replace it with an adequate bottom-up strategy. The ulterior reason is just that complexities of intentionality are said to be dismissible in principle (the argument merely defers in the direction of Quine's and Davidson's views), *and* that the idiom we begin with – that clearly favors a top-down strategy – is ultimately a mere *façon de parler*, a dispensable idiom (like our talk of *persons* (Dennett, (1969)), though it does introduce the range of phenomena that the final bottom-up language must be able to redescribe and explain. It is for this reason that Dennett is quite explicit – against Fodor, for instance – that *if* persons, sub-personal homunculi or similar 'agents' described in intentionally complex ways are not ultimately dismissed, our would-be psychology is 'doomed to circularity or infinite regress', is no scientific psychology at all.

Dennett's argument manages to array, in a dialectical form, a number of the key competing strategies of our own time, quite apart from his own strong adherence to extensionalism and the unity of science program. We may for instance distinguish between a 'provisional' and an 'ultimate' use of top-down and bottom-up strategies. Clearly it is only the 'ultimate' use that is programatically decisive: Dennett himself is a provisional top-down strategist *because* he is an ultimate bottom-up man; whereas Chomsky and Fodor are, ultimately, top-down theorists. (These distinctions of course must be relativized to what these and other authors have actually defended: it is entirely possible that Fodor, say, might be, even 'more' ultimately, a bottom-up theorist.) So nothing very much hangs on favoring, provisionally, either the top-down or bottom-up strategy. What is decisive is whether one concedes or denies the asymmetry between the two.

If we see matters this way, then there are, as *ultimate* strategies, two principal sorts of bottom-up moves, each of which may appear in a great variety of forms and each of which may be linked in a great variety of ways with 'provisional' strategies. Thus, for example, among Anglo-American philosophies of psychology (as well as in empirical psychologics of a sympathetic sort), there are many theorists who subscribe to the general dictum that – whatever the difficulties involved in dispensing with the idiom (our idiom) that admits persons, their mental and cognitive states, their linguistically and intentionally qualified behavior and functions – we may in principle, and hopefully in practice, ultimately *eliminate* all such discourse from the science of psychology. Perhaps the most explicit and ramified recent version of this thesis appears in the views of the influential American philosopher, Wilfrid Sellars (1963). It also appears, in a variety of forms, in Carnap, Davidson, Paul Feyerabend (1963), Dennett, and, quite energetically in the last few years, in the views of Paul Churchland (1979) and Stephen Stich (1983) – which in a way hark back to Sellars's thesis. Stich for example is ready, now, to scrap the picturesque 'folk psychology' that favors discourse about persons and the rest; Churchland would do so ultimately but not yet. So once again rather in the same sense in which we have characterized Dennett as a decidedly bottom-up theorist provisionally prepared to proceed top-down, there is often very little to distinguish one eliminative program from another, except in terms of effective timing and local preference. If we remind ourselves of Hull's program and of Skinner's ambivalence about elimination and paraphrase we oblige ourselves to concede that not very much has changed in this particular regard. Tolman (1958) for example, particularly with regard to 'intervening variables', is seen to be ambivalent in a more profound sense than Skinner.

By and large, the regularly favored version of the botttom-up strategy (in the 'ultimate' sense) has simply been some version of physicalism. But in recent years, bottom-up strategies have taken on a variety of quite different forms: first, with respect to *what* is supposed to be the fundamental – or relatively fundamental – stratum of the psychological domain; second, with respect to *how* best to proceed, now, with regard to whatever may (at some later time) prove to be that stratum. Current philosophers of psychology, particularly those that (one way or another) are intended to promote something akin to the unity of science model, have generated quite sophisticated versions of bottom-up strategies of these two sorts. They are all of course subject to the general objections already summarized; but it is easy to fail to grasp the line of development they favor, and they remain distinctly vigorous, particularly in the United States.

The principle contrast, with respect to *what* is the relatively fundamental stratum of the psychological domain, tends to be disputed (which may well be too strong a term) between the *physicalists* and what we may call the *Leibnizians*. Theorists like Hull and Skinner (and less interestingly, Watson) and, among philosophers, Carnap, Feigl, and Davidson may serve to fix our sense of the possible varieties of physicalism. Chomsky – hence, also, Fodor – is an exemplar of the Leibnizian thesis. Roughly, by 'Leibnizian' (a term of art), one means a theorist who treats the fundamental stratum of a range of psychologically pertinent phenomena as indissolubly informational or language-like. Thus, insofar as he characterizes as *genetic* the determinants of the universal or species-wide 'deep grammar' of natural languages, Chomsky functions as a Leibnizian. Similarly, Fodor, who treats our conceptual powers as essentially innate (protolinguistic, as analogues of predicates), is also a Leibnizian. (Clearly, contemporary speculations about the possible irreducibility of biological 'codes' suggest the larger context for the revival of Leibnizian theories.)

For purposes of contrast, Piaget may be thought to be more inclined to adopt a top-down strategy than a bottom-up one; if so, then there is much more profound disagreement between Chomsky and Piaget than their well-known debate suggests. Another recent Leibnizian, perhaps the most systematic currently, among American theorists, is Fred Dretske (1981), who explicitly subordinates language and knowledge to a deeper informational stratum in nature itself, to which language and knowledge subsequently are to relate. As Dretske rather neatly puts the point: 'In the beginning there was information. The word came later.'

In general, the Leibnizians are persuaded that a strong physicalism of a Carnapian or similar sort will prove inadequate for psychology and the human sciences. This, for example, may well be the point of dispute between Fodor and Dennett. But the Leibnizians may also be 'provisionalists' (as Fodor often seems to be and as Dretske definitely is not). In any case, there are well-known difficulties confronting the Leibnizian thesis, since the proper description and explanation of the informational or quasi-linguistic properties imputed to the real world are normally not satisfactorily provided. Are they introduced heuristically, for instance, or are they intended quite literally as characterizations of nature? Part of the problem rests with the fact (against Dretske) that information seems to be modelled only linguistically – in fact, propositionally. So it is very difficult to maintain that the fundamental atoms (or monads) of the natural world or of that sector that comprises psychology (or biology) just are informational or quasi-linguistic. It may be that, thus construed, the Leibnizian view simply reads back into nature – perhaps for the sake of an adjusted unity model – precisely what anti-unity psychologists and philosophers specify via top-down strategies. There seems to be little doubt that Chomsky's strategy is very much like that.

This convergence between bottom-up Leibnizians and top-down theorists who emphasize the emergent, *sui generis* nature of language may well provide the best clue we have to the various forms of so-called *functionalism*. For functionalism isolates an intentional, teleological, informational, coded, semiotic or similar set of abstract traits assignable in psychological or cognitive contexts, that are distinct from physical or biological traits and that are not reducible to the latter. The entire orientation of AI simulation favors functionalism to this extent at least. It has been championed in certain much-discussed early papers of Hilary Putnam's (1975, vol. 2), though Putnam no longer subscribes to the doctrine as thus formulated.

Functionalism is a troublesome thesis to specify, because it is often not fully explicated. It may be advocated in a heuristic or realist sense; and, even where construed in a realist sense, it may be thought to designate properties merely abstracted from more complex properties from which they cannot actually be disengaged, or it may be thought to designate independent properties. Where functionalist properties are taken as abstract, real and independent, one is committed to a form of *dualism* distinctive of the new cognitive sciences. This, for instance, is the decisive conceptual weakness of Putnam's early position. Where functionalism is intended in a heuristic sense – possibly in both Fodor and Dennett – there is usually a strong tendency to favor an ultimate physicalism. The merit of a realist-minded Leibnizian is just that he means to oppose the adequacy of physicalism (by introducing Leibnizian 'monads' at a fundamental level); hence he is opposed to construing psychological properties (or those central to the cognitive and informational sciences) as independent of physical or biological properties. This, for example, may be the distinctive strength of Dretske's thesis. Put more affirmatively, functionalism is at best a partial or heuristic version of a thesis that postulates *psychological* (or biological) properties as *incarnate* properties, that is, as emergent, indissolubly complex properties that exhibit both physical or biological aspects *and* informational, intentional, linguistic or similar aspects (often and viably abstracted as functional but not separable – see, for instance, Margolis, 1984a, 1984b).

The theory of emergent incarnate properties – of functionalism thus construed – is clearly linked with the fortunes of the unity model. In bottom-up strategies, as in Dretske and Chomsky, it appears to favor an extension of the unity model. But its plausibility is put into question, once we grasp that, as fundamenta, the 'coded' monads (genetic, in Chomsky's view; ubiquitously 'natural', in Dretske's) are both unsatisfactorily specified and, insofar as they are characterized, are characterized in a way that is distinctly dependent, conceptually, on linguistic models – that is, on models that, on the hypothesis, must be assigned phenomena themselves constructed from these fundamenta. In this sense, the Leibnizian thesis is incompletely analyzed – and perhaps ultimately untenable. But the weakness of the Leibnizian view is just the strength of its top-down counterpart, since the description of complex linguistic and cultural phenomena need not be supposed to be reducible to fundamenta of either the physicalist or Leibnizian sort. As we have already remarked, only a descending continuum of explanation is available to any top-down strategy that concedes (however provisionally) the emergent, *sui generis* nature of language and of whatever emergently depends on its human exercise.

It is of course not unreasonable to suppose that we are far from being able to formulate the relative fundamenta of psychology and the human and cognitive sciences. Bottom-up theorists who incline to the Leibnizian view tend to mute the serious methodological question of the *homonomic* nature of science itself (see Davidson, 1970), that is, the question of whether the laws of a domain may be expressed in terms of the same basic descriptive vocabulary suited to the entire range of phenomena of that designated domain – say, physicalistic laws covering a domain described in entirely physicalistic terms. (A homonomic domain is said to be a *closed* domain.) For, it is not clear whether the introduction of Leibnizian phenomena or the introduction of Leibnizian-like laws ranging over physical phenomena is or is not to be construed homonomically. Chomsky would extend the use of 'physical' so that it was; Dennett seems to believe that it cannot be. On the top-down view that favors the irreducibility of the linguistic and the cultural, *the homonomic (or closed) nature of the physical sciences is decisively breached.* That is assuredly the point of principal contention between the advocates of the unity model and its opponents.

But if we do not essay to fix the fundamenta of psychology, then, at least for an influential group of bottom-up theorists, it may still be possible to fix certain formal or syntactic constraints on *any and all* viable theories of the domain. Here, certain technical developments in formal logic are thought to provide the required direction. We have already touched very briefly on Davidson's extension of Tarski's theory of truth to natural languages and the sciences; and we have noted the fact that Fodor uses Davidson's extension to provide a formal account of innate concepts along extensionalist lines. Roughly, to be clear about the issue: on Fodor's view, to have or understand a concept is to know the conditions (sufficient, or necessary and sufficient) on which it may be truthfully applied to the entire range of things to which it applies. This is said to be an *extensional* account of concepts – or of predicates – which is certainly close to what Fodor has in mind. Its gravest difficulties concern the following: that there may be co-extensive concepts (or predicates) that differ in meaning despite the fact that they have the same extension or range of application (at least in real-time terms); that no one can be said to understand concepts or predicates in this sense; and that it is utterly counterintuitive to suppose that we are innately endowed with such a 'knowledge' with respect to conceptual fundamenta. (Generally, then, these objections constitute a return to the intensional puzzles of inten/ionality.)

The underlying formal commitment is a commitment to the universal adequacy of an extensional syntax for all natural languages *and* to the confidence that this may be determined independently of the contingent history of any empirical science – *a fortiori* independently of empirical psychology. *This*, ultimately, explains why so many among Anglo-American psychologists and philosophers of psychology (including the intuitive but quite informal views of Skinner as well as the extremely bold but better informed theories of, say, Sellars and Davidson and Stich) dismiss, as old-fashioned and superannuated, the standard vocabulary and explanatory apparatus of persons, languages, cultures, practices, meanings, histories, interpretations, intentions and the like. We may concede on intuitive grounds that *any* finite string or sequence of 'intelligent' behavior or processing can be simulated by a machine that is provided with an extensionalized program (a program that accords with extensionalist views of logic). This is the point of the famous puzzle regarding the universal competence of Turing machines and of the so-called Turing Test of intelligence (by which a machine may pass as

46 JOSEPH MARGOLIS

intelligent – see Boden, 1977; Dreyfus, 1972/79; Putnam, 1975, vol. 2; Searle, 1980; Turing, 1950).

We have already had occasion to remark that Quine's use of the extensionalist strategy is defective precisely because it is applied *to* interpreted natural languages on the presumption that it must be antecedently suited to them. The same may be argued with respect to psychology. But here the deficiency is raised to a virtue. No one, however, has shown that it is possible to reduce extensionally the entire play of natural language. This was just the point of Tarski's demurrer regarding his own formal program; and it is the analogue of an objection to a powerful supplement to that program – known as Church's thesis (Church, 1936): roughly, that if there is an effective or formal proof for an argument or computation or the like (addition, for example), then that proof is recursive. (Church's thesis is, obviously, a boon for the extensional treatment of the AI simulation of psychological processes, construed functionally.) Also, of course, we now see precisely why physicalism is so much admired by the unity of science theorists: the replacement of a psychological idiom by a physical one is meant to facilitate a strongly or completely extensional treatment of critical predicates.

The double issue to bear in mind, however, is this: (a) the universal adequacy of an extensional syntax for suitably formalized languages cannot as such determine whether natural languages exhibit similar structures (Tarski): and (b) the universal adequacy of an extensional syntax for simulating any *finite* segment of a natural language (or surrogate) cannot as such determine whether the actual, indefinitely open-ended, historically contingent use of a natural language exhibits as such a structure that can also be similarly simulated or mapped. The affirmative position on the second question is both the high hope of AI theory and the explicit thesis that Davidson favors (1984). But the crucial fact is that, despite all insistence to the contrary, the issues raised by both (a) and (b) are *empirical*. Because they are, this most recent strategy regarding *how* we should now proceed, assuming a bottom-up approach in which we cannot yet see our way to positing the required fundamenta, is basically flawed or at least open to an entirely responsible opposition. It is Davidson's view (and Stich follows him in this) that the empirical vocabulary and explanatory efforts of psychology can be known in advance to be amenable to an extensionalist treatment (which, thus far, is equivocal in the respect just noted) and, furthermore, an extensionalist treatment that will ultimately favor theories in accord with a strong version of the unity of science model (which is simply gratuitous).

Concluding remarks

We have now completed our survey on its critical side. We must add a little regarding the possible directions the new psychologies and philosophies of psychology are likely to take. All the predictable novelties may be linked to a single theme that we have as yet not emphasized. We must remind ourselves that, on the foregoing argument (better, on the foregoing sketch of an argument), *the new psychologies are bound to be top-down, committed to a strong view of the emergence of language and culture as* sui generis *phenonomena, committed to that version of methodological individualism that concedes the irreducibility of the societal to the individualistic, committed to construing psychological properties as incarnate (hence, linking biology and culture), opposed to the unity of science program though not to whatever unity may be associated with a descending continuum of explanation, committed to the rejection of a homonomic reading of the sciences unless that reading is applied to the most complex order of phenomena, and committed to the intensional complexity of intentional contexts.* That is already to say a great deal. A psychology that meets these conditions would be radically different from the exemplars that have prevailed primarily in the Anglo-American tradition and rather less opposed to those that have prevailed in the Continental. As already remarked, however, such a psychology need not resist any of the achievements belonging to the exemplars of the first sort. This should remind us of the alternative ways of construing the use of the unity model itself.

The large theme that we have barely hinted at, that will undoubtedly color any fresh psychologies meeting the constraints listed just above, is the theme of history, of what in fact may be called *historicism* – meaning by that term not the now pejoratively received doctrine associated (debatably) with Hegel and Marx and with much of nineteenth-century histories and theories of history, but the doctrine that human existence is radically historical without there being, in temporal terms or from a God's-eye view, any purpose, telos, or discernible direction toward which human history may be said to be moving. This is the point of Popper's well-known criticism of (nineteenth-century) historicism (1961): but it may be fairly disputed whether Hegel or Marx is well served by the charge. It is in any case a charge utterly alien to the thesis here intended. For the purpose of linking the issue with the fortunes of psychology (and of the theory of science), we may say that the entire societal orientation within which individual psychology is to be examined is itself *subject to radically contingent historical change.* This may well be the most heterodox element of the new psychologies. Its direct consequence is, quite simply put, that the study of the psychology of individuals is inseparable from the study of their societal milieux and that *that study is not and cannot be the study of an essential human nature*. The theme of the new psychologies, we may venture, will be, that man's 'nature' is his history.

We must resist, here, pursuing that theme. What is important to realize, however, is that, with very few exceptions, the principal direction Anglo-American psychology and philosophy of psychology has taken is indifferent or opposed to both the societal and the historicist dimensions of human existence. Those themes surely must be traced to Hegel and Marx preeminently; in current Continental thought, they have become particularly influential through the views of such thinkers (seemingly far removed from the professional study of psychology) as Nietzsche, Heidegger, Gadamer and Habermas. But if we add *the commitment to historicism* to our previous list (and whatever that may be judged to entail), then we may fairly claim to have identified the salient features of now-emerging psychologies and theories of science and of the gathering efforts of those that are sure to come.

REFERENCES

Where two dates are given after an author's name (for example, Popper, K. R. 1956/1982), the first indicates the year of original publication and the second the edition referred to in the text whose publication details are cited here.

Armstrong, D. M. 1968: *A Material Theory of the Mind*. London: Routledge and Kegan Paul.
Armstrong, D. M. 1973: *Belief, Truth and Knowledge*. Cambridge: Cambridge University Press.
Austin, J. L. 1962: *How to Do Things with Words*. Oxford: Clarendon.
Bakhtin, M. M. 1981: *The Dialogic Imagination*, translated by C. Emerson and M. Holquist, Austin, Texas: University of Texas Press.
Bennett, J. 1964: *Rationality*. London: Routledge and Kegan Paul.
Block, Ned. (Ed.) 1980: *Readings in Philosophy of Psychology*, vol. 1 Cambridge, Harvard University Press.
Boden, M. A. 1977: *Artificial Intelligence and Natural Man*. New York, NY: Basic Books.
Bourdieu, P. 1972/1977: *Outline of a Theory of Practice*, translated by R. Nice, Cambridge: Cambridge University Press.
Brentano, Franz 1874/1973: The distinction between mental and physical

phenomena. In O. Kraus (ed.), *Psychology from an Empirical Standpoint* (English edition, ed. L. L. McAlister), London: Routledge and Kegan Paul.

Bunge, M. 1977a: Emergence and the mind. *Neuroscience*, 9.

Bunge, M. 1977b: Levels of reduction. *American Journal of Physiology*, 103.

Carnap, R. 1932–33/1959: Psychology in physical langauge, translated by G. Schick. In A. J. Ayer (ed.), *Logical Positivism*. Glencoe, Ill.: Free Press.

Cartwright, N. 1983: *How the Laws of Physics Lie*. Oxford: Oxford University Press.

Causey, R. L. 1977: *Unity of Science*. Dordrecht, Holland: Reidel.

Chomsky, N. 1959: Review of B. F. Skinner, Verbal behavior. *Language*, 35.

Chomsky, N. 1980: *Rules and Representations*. New York, NY: Columbia University Press.

Church, A. 1936: An unsolvable problem of elementary number theory. *American Journal of Mathematics*, 58.

Churchland, P. M. 1979: *Scientific Realism and the Philosophy of Mind*. Cambridge: Cambridge University Press.

Davidson, D. 1970: Mental events. In L. Foster and J. W. Swanson (eds)., *Experience and Theory*, Amherst, Mass.: University of Massachusetts Press.

Davidson, D. 1984: *Inquiries into Truth and Interpretation*. Oxford: Clarendon.

Dennett, D. C. 1969: *Content and Consciousness*. London: Routledge and Kegan Paul.

Dennett, D. C. 1978: *Brainstorms*. Montgomery, VT: Bradford Books.

Dretske, F. I. 1981: *Knowledge and the Flow of Information*. Cambridge, Mass.: MIT Press.

Dreyfus, H. L. 1972/1979: *What Computers Can't Do*, revised edition, New York, NY: Harper and Row.

Feigl, H. 1958/1967: *The 'Mental' and the 'Physical'. The essay and a postscript*. Minneapolis: University of Minnesota Press.

Feyerabend, P. F. 1963: Materialism and the mind-body problem. *Review of Metaphysics*, 17.

Fodor, J. A. 1975: *The Language of Thought*. New York, NY: Crowell.

Fodor, J. A. 1983: *The Modularity of Mind*. Cambridge, MIT Press.

Foucault, M. 1966/1970: *The Order of Things*. New York, NY: Random House.

Harré, R. 1979: *Social Being*. Totowa, NJ: Rowman and Littlefield.

Harré, R. 1984: *Personal Being*. Cambridge, Mass.: Harvard University Press.

Hempel, C. G. 1965: *Aspects of Scientific Explanation*. New York, NY: Free Press.

Hjelmslev L. 1943/1961: *Prolegomena to a Theory of Language*, revised edition, translated by F. J. Whitfield, Madison, WI: University of Wisconsin Press.

Husserl, E. 1954/1970: *The Crisis of European Sciences and Transcendental Phenomenology*, translated by D. Carr, Evanston, Ill.: Northwestern University Press.

Margolis J. 1984a: *Philosophy of Psychology*. Englewood Cliffs, NJ: Prentice-Hall.

Margolis, J. 1984b: *Culture and Cultural Entities*. Dordrecht, Holland: Reidel.

Mead, G. H. 1934: *Mind, Self and Society*. Chicago, Ill.: University of Chicago Press.

Merleau-Ponty, M. 1942/1963: *The Structure of Behavior*, translated by A. L. Fisher, Boston, Mass.: Beacon.

Nelson, R. J. 1969: Behaviorism is false. *Journal of Philosophy*, 66.

Nelson, R. J. 1982: *The Logic of Mind*. Dordrecht, Holland: Reidel.

Neurath, O. 1932–33/1959: Protocol sentences, translated by G. Schick, in A. J. Ayer (ed.), *Logical Positivism*. Glencoe: Free Press.

Neurath, O. et al (eds.) 1955: *International Encyclopedia of Unified Science* (vol. 1, Pts. 1–2). Chicago, Ill.: University of Chicago Press.

Oppenheim, P. and Putnam, H 1958.: Unity of science as a working hypothesis. In H. Feigl et al (eds), *Minnesota Studies in the Philosophy of Science*, Vol. 2, Minneapolois, MN: University of Minnesota Press.

Piattelli-Palmarini, M. (ed.) 1980: *Language and Learning: the debate between Jean Piaget and Noam Chomsky*. Cambridge, Mass.: Harvard University Press.

Popper, K. R. 1950: *The Open Society and its Enemies*. Princeton, NJ: Princeton University Press.

Popper, K. R. 1956/1982: *The Open Universe*. Totowa, NJ: Rowman and Littlefield.

Popper, K. R. 1956/1983: *Realism and the Aim of Science*. Totowa, NJ: Rowman and Littlefield.

Popper, K. R. 1961: *The Poverty of Historicism*, 3rd edition, London: Routledge and Kegan Paul.

Putnam, H. 1975: *Philosophical Papers*, vol. 2 Cambridge: Cambridge University Press.

Quine, W. V. 1953: Two dogmas of empiricism. In *From a Logical Point of View*. Cambridge, Mass.: Harvard University Press.

Quine. W. V. 1960: *Word and Object* Cambridge, Mass.: MIT Press.

Rorty, R. 1979: *Philosophy and the Mirror of Nature*. Princeton, NJ: Princeton University Press.

Rosch, E. 1973,: Natural categories. *Cognitive Psychology, 4*.

Saussure, F. de 1916/1959: *Course in General Linguistics*, edited by C. Bally et al., translated by W. Baskin, New York, NY: McGraw-Hill.

Searle, J. R. 1980: Minds, brain and programs. *Behavioral and Brain Sciences, 3*.

Sellars, W. 1963: Philosophy and the scientific image of man. In *Science, Perception and Reality*. London: Routledge and Kegan Paul.

Skinner, B. F. 1953: *Science and Human Behavior*. New York, NY: Macmillan.

Skinner, B. F. 1957: *Verbal Behavior* New York, NY: Appleton-Century-Crofts.

Skinner, B. F. 1964: Behaviorism at fifty. In T. W. Wann (ed.), *Behaviorism and Phenomenology*, Chicago, University of Chicago Press.

Smart, J. J. C. 1959/1962: Sensations and brain processes (rev.). In V. C. Chappell (ed.), *The Philosophy of Mind*, Englewood Cliffs, NJ: Prentice-Hall.

Stich S. P. 1983: *From Folk Psychology to Cognitive Science*. Cambridge, Mass.: MIT Press.

Tarski, A. 1944: The semantic conception of truth. *Philosophy and Phenomenological Research, 4*.

Tarski, A. 1956/1983: The concept of truth in formalized languages. In *Logic, Semantics, Metamathematics*, 2nd edition, translated by J. H. Woodger, Indianapolis, IN: Hackett Publishing Co.
Tolman, E. C. 1958: *Behavior and Psychological Man*. Berkeley, Cal.: University of California Press.
Turing, A. M. 1950: Computing machinery and intelligence. *Mind*, 59.
van Fraassen, B. C. 1980: *The Scientific Image*. Oxford: Oxford University Press.
Vygotsky, L. S. 1934/1962: *Thought and Language*, translated by E. Hanfmann and G. Vakar, Cambridge, Mass.: MIT Press.
Vygotsky, L. S. 1978: *Mind in Society*, edited by M. Cole et al., translated by A. R. Luria et al., Cambridge, Mass. and London: Harvard University Press.
Watson, J. B. 1913/1963: Psychology as the behaviorist views it. In W. Dennes (ed.), *Readings in the History of Psychology*. New York, NY: Appleton-Century-Crofts.
Watson, J. B. 1925: *Behaviorism* London: Kegan Paul, Trench and Trubner.

3

Whither Psychology?

Peter T. Manicas

The genesis of 'experimental psychology'

Introduction

To make a convincing case for a coherent view of the many-roomed mansion we today call 'psychology' will hardly be easy. There are two related reasons for this. First, as everyone knows, there is the obvious proliferation of sub-disciplines and the ambiguous relations which have long existed between the more 'applied' branches of psychology and the more 'theoretical' or 'experimental' branches – with no real hope in sight of getting all this together. Psychologists, facing monumentally complicated problems, practical and theoretical, are prepared to use whatever serves the problem at hand. Second, there is a history behind the proliferation of psychologies. For quite good reasons, academic psychology has assumed tasks that very likely it cannot accomplish. And for equally good reasons, it has been institutionalized in terms of manifestly untenable beliefs. But if those beliefs are embedded in the training and certification of practitioners, they need not actually be acknowledged. Indeed, if they were, and if I am correct about their untenability, they would have to *change*. Let me list here what I take these beliefs to be, without explication or defense:

1　That the commonsense, meaningful perceptual world is a datum for psychological inquiry, not merely a provisional starting place for such inquiry – not itself requiring psychological explanation. People 'see' trees, even if they must 'learn' to call them 'trees'.

2   This perceptual world – the world of 'experience' – though shared by individuals, is not essentially social. (This is part of the foregoing, as we shall see.)
3   The mind-body problem is insoluble; but irrelevant.
4   Science has as its task the discovery and confirmation of lawful uniformities, construed as Humean regularities. These enable us to explain by subsumption.
5   The goal of psychology is the explanation of behavior – even though, of course, it is acknowledged that many 'variables' enter into this.
6   Explanation and prediction are symmetrical; prediction and control are coterminous.

This essay adopts two strategies. In the first part ('The genesis of experimental psychology'), I make the effort to recover, if but sketchily, the key elements in the institutionalization of psychology as a science. It is my hope that this effort will help clarify the foregoing 'assumptions' and help to expose them as the underlying assumptions of prevailing practice that they are. I argue that there have been four conceptual 'turns' that have been crucial: the bifurcation of 'mind' and 'matter' and their subsequent relegation to the realm of the 'metaphysical'; the rejection of a Helmholtzian alternative to anti-metaphysical 'empiricisms'; the rejection of a Wundtian conception of mind as social; and the affirmation, promoted for epistemological and practical reasons, of an Americanized conception of psychology as the science of behavior. The second part ('A limited program') then, addresses these assumptions more directly, and seeks to articulate and defend an alternative understanding of psychology as a science.

The development of British 'psychology'

We can distinguish two more or less independent strands in the development of the idea of 'psychology', British and German. The background of the British tradition is Locke's *Essay Concerning the Human Understanding* (1690). It stimulated Hartley's *Observations on Man* (1749), a psychophysical effort to integrate Newton's theory of the aether with Locke's associationism. Sensation causes 'vibrations' which in turn leave a 'vestige' which becomes the material for the complicated 'ideas' which are characteristic of human understanding. Joseph Priestley (1733–1805) exorcised the 'vibrations' part of the story and James Mill, familiar not just with Hartley's work, but with what had transpired in-between, including Hume's analysis of causality, pursued what has come to be called 'British associationism'. In the nineteenth century, this empiricist direction, in J. S. Mill and Alexander Bain, the founder of the journal *Mind* (1876), was strongly anti-metaphysical and anti-sociological. We can see this clearly in Mill's influential account in his *Logic* (first edition, 1843).

When working on the *Logic*, Mill had been reading Comte, whose 'positive philosophy' had argued for a hierarchy of sciences. There was no place in that hierarchy for psychology. As Kant had argued, psychology was metaphysical (Leary, 1982). Having no patience for metaphysics, Comte held that mind and ego were useless abstractions, remnants of our previous 'metaphysical stage'. His associate Laurent, writing in 1826, had put the matter exactly in noting that while physiology 'stops where the phenomena are wanting, psychology abandons observation to mount by the inductive path to causality, to substance' (Boas, 1924, p. 282). That 'causality' and 'substance' were metaphysical, everyone could agree: Hume, Kant, Comte and Mill.

But Comte was no 'reductionist.' For him, physiology was *not* psychology. Animals, like humans, perceive, feel, and are purposeful. They were not, however, social. Physiology was a science in the hierarchy of sciences, right below the new human science, the science of 'sociology', the science of man as a social being. As humans were everywhere social and were so *in virtue of* social phenomena, one could explain human nature by understanding society, but not conversely.

Mill agreed with Comte that if psychology was to be a science, it had to rid itself of metaphysics, and he agreed that physiology was a science. Yet Comte had gone too far in eliminating the possibility of a psychology. Mill's problem was to give some non-metaphysical and non-socially produced content to the human part of 'human nature'.

He did this by arguing that 'the laws of the mind . . . comprise the universal or abstract portion of the philosophy of human nature' (*Logic*, bk VI, ch. 5). Of course, one had to distinguish 'mind' from its 'sensible manifestations'. Inquiry into the former was metaphysics. Further, 'states of mind are immediately caused either by other states of mind or by a state of the body' (ch. 4). The former fall under the laws of the mind and constitute the proper province of 'psychology'. The account of sensation, however, belongs to physiology since sensation always has 'for its proximate cause some affection of the portion of our frame called the nervous system'. Accordingly, Mill eliminated from psychology everything but the 'laws of the succession of states of mind'. For him, even 'ethology', the 'science of the formation of character' is to be distinguished from psychology, because, with Comte, this is fundamentally a problem for a social science. Mill wanted both a universal non-physiological psychology and social human nature – a posture, I take it, that would today be widely subscribed to. Yet Mill could believe this *coherently*, since for him – in contrast to current views – psychology was not the science of behavior. Ethology, a social science, might shed light on socially produced human character. Given this *and* and the biography of a person, one might *begin* to explain his or her behavior.

The German tradition of 'psychology'

The alternative German tradition was spawned by Leibniz. It will be wise, here, to disentangle three components. The first is distinctly Leibnizian, generated in specific response to Locke. Its permanent legacy to the German tradition was the idea of an active and unitive mind, having a capacity for instantaneous apperception. Versions of this are to be found in Kant of course, in Johann Herbart (1776–1841) and in Wundt (1832–1920). The second is the post-Kantian historicist strain of German Idealism, in which 'subjective mind' is transcended in favor of an 'objective' or Absolute Mind. The crucial empirical implication of this – and crucial it is indeed – is that mind is social and historical. Wundt's ten-volume *Volkerpsychologie* (1900–20) represents the culmination of this. Let it be said that there is nothing in the British psychological tradition comparable to either of these ideas. Also, to anticipate: it was the British tradition that determined the course of modern academic psychology.

The third element of the German tradition is a physical and physiological theme. In the continental and British traditions this derived ultimately from early modern physical science, Newtonian and Cartesian. Kurt Danziger has recently reminded us that 'British psychophysiology of the mid-Victorian period constitutes an almost forgotten chapter in the history of psychology' (Danziger, 1982, p. 119). The fact that it was 'almost forgotten' is important, for this confirms the impression, supported on other grounds, that it had all but disappeared. In part, it was forgotten because of the powerful development of psychophysiology that emerged at mid-century, in Germany. Influenced by *Naturphilosophie*, the Germans, Johannes Müller, Purkinje, E. H. Weber, Volkmann and in the next generation, Vierodt, Donders, Aubert, Fechner ('psycho-physics'), Helmholtz and finally Wundt, were unabashedly 'philosophical' and at the same time fully committed to the development of experimental techniques. For present purposes, three figures are central: Helmholtz, Wundt and Mach.

Helmholtz's alternative

Hermann von Helmholtz (1821–94) 'was a very great scientist, one of the greatest of the nineteenth century'. So writes E. G. Boring at the beginning of his chapter devoted to examining Helmholtz's contribution to 'experimental psychology'. An army surgeon in Berlin, Helmholtz read his famous paper on the conservation of energy before the *Physikalische Gesellschaft* in 1847, became professor of physiology and general pathology at Königsberg in 1849, invented the ophthalmoscope in 1851, published his *Handbuch der physiologischen Optic* (vol. 1) in 1856 and his *Tonempfindungen* in 1863. He was called to the chair of physics in Berlin in 1871 and continued to publish and lecture on physics, philosophy and psychophysiology until his death in 1894. All this is well-known and acknowledged. What is less frequently noted is his idea of psychology as a general epistemology.

Briefly, Helmholtz held that what we can know is circumscribed by the nature of our sense organs and central nervous system. But this was not an empiricism as Mill had understood it or a Kantianism with a Transcendental Ego. It was, rather, a kind of physiological Kantianism in which the structures of experience are complexly linked to the functioning of our sense organs, 'unconscious inferences' (*unbewusste Schluss*) of the central nervous system (CNS), and inputs from the 'external world'.

On this view, 'experience' is a 'sign', not an 'image' or 'reflection' of the external world. As Mandelbaum writes, 'according to Helmholtz, the difference between languages as systems of signs, and sense perception as a system of signs, is that the system of our sensations is not arbitrary, but is in fact a universal language of which there are not diverse families or differing dialects' (Mandelbaum, 1971, p. 293). This means that we must distinguish between sensations of sight and perceptions of sight. The latter are 'interpretations' which depend upon unconscious inferencing. This view implies, moreover, that a subject/object distinction is to be preserved, but the 'object' is not the experienced object, say, a tree or a mountain, since such an 'object' is the product of sensory imput from the physical world as processed in the CNS, an insight preserved in twentieth-century Gestalt psychology, but otherwise nowhere evident.

Finally, and crucially, as Locke had held – but not Hume or the tradition which followed him – causality is rightly construed as the generative power of an object, not phenomenally manifest features of events nor invariances that, as Mach would argue, are only 'mathematical functions'. It was just this view of causality, a realist view, which allowed for a causal theory of perception. That is, the 'objects' at the object-end, and the mediated 'objects' of the ordered phenomenal field, are known only in virtue of the causal powers of 'things' in the world. Both are known only inferentially, the former as the theoretical entities of physical theory and the latter as outcomes of the unconscious inferences of the CNS.

This must not be missed. Just as the Cartesian destruction of naive realism made a *theoretical* physics possible, it seems to have made a theoretical psychology impossible. There seemed to be no way to close the causal gap between 'objects' in the world and the contents of consciousness. Indeed, if causes are constant conjunctions established in experience, 'psychology' *must* be either metaphysical or 'associationist'. Helmholtz saw otherwise. For him, the fundamental problem was not to explain, *per* metaphysics, the nature of mind or, *per* Mill and the associationists, the laws of the mind – independently of physiology – but rather to see how it was that 'information' flowing to the 'mind' could issue in meaningful experience. The program was to involve not only a theory of perception but, of necessity, a theory of cognition. As we shall see, it was, despite being almost completely dead-ended in the first decade of this century, notably consistent with a social theory of knowledge.

While I have little doubt that this was Helmholtz's program, Helmholtz himself never treated it as a program for psychology. We must remember that, at this time, psychology had neither an assigned domain nor an institutional location. Helmholtz rarely used the term, 'psychology,' and when he did, the term usually signified what we now call 'philosophy'. He thought of himself as contributing to 'sensory physiology' and to 'epistemology' (in a non-technical sense). While he would have admitted that epistemology has a normative or regulative dimension (in Kant's sense), it was not to be viewed as a distinct scientific concern.

The nativism/empiricism debate

There are, of course, some genuine difficulties in Helmholtz's notion. But it is important to see that Helmholtz's program was buried not because of the emergence of a superior scientific alternative, but for philosophical and institutional reasons. One issue worth spending a moment on is the famous 'nativism/empiricism' debate.

This argument was not, as Boring would have it, between Kant/Fichte idealism on the one hand and the British psychology of the two Mills on the other – at least as these are usually understood – because Helmholtz sided with neither (Pastore, 1974). It is not easy to paraphrase the issues; accordingly, let me quote from Helmholtz. We need one of his terms of art, 'local signs', understood as spatially different retinal locations of the same sensation, e.g., a particular shade of red. According to Helmholtz, then,

> The difference between the two opposing views is as follows: The empirical theory [Helmholtz's] regards the local signs . . . as signs whose signification must be learned, and is actually learned, in order to arrive at a knowledge of the external world.
> It is not necessary to suppose any kind of correspondence between these local signs and the actual differences of spatial location they signify. The nativist theory, on the other hand, supposes that the local signs are direct perceptions of actual differences in space, both in their nature and in their magnitude. (Helmholtz, 1971, p. 197)

There is, here, a difference between what is 'learned' and what is 'innate', but this difference is posed in the dispute between Helmholtz and Hering in terms of *physiology*. For both, Kant had been *naturalized*. On the nativist view, 'certain perceptual images of space [are] produced directly by an inborn mechanism provided certain nerve fibres [are] stimulated.' The Kantian 'ego' is already physiologized. On this view no learning is necessary for our spatial intuitions, since there is an immediate 'correspondence' between the retinal 'sign' and the objects of the structured world, a world which is not experienced but is the *cause* of experience. On Helmholtz's view, by contrast, 'none of our sensations give us anything more than signs for external objects . . . and we learn how to interpret these signs only through experience and practice. For example, the perception of differences in spatial location can be attained only through movement; in the field of vision it depends upon our experience of the movements of the eye' (1971 p. 196).

Helmholtz's 'empirical' theory does stand against Kant and is in the spirit of Locke, but it accords with Locke's spirit not because it is phenomenalist but because it is *realist*. For that reason it is not a version of Millian empiricism. The argument between Hering and Helmholtz presupposes that there is a reality that is independent of our experience, which is causally implicated in perception. The nativist view, argues

Helmholtz, 'assumes that the laws of mental operations are in pre-existing harmony with those of the outer world', a magical dualistic harmony. It is, accordingly, an unexplained miracle that our perceptual signs 'correspond' to the external world. But on Helmholtz's view of the matter, 'correlations' are learned: as in learning a language, where we learn to connect wholly arbitrary signs to what is signified – and do this quite 'naturally' – we similarly learn to 'interpret' our perceptual signs as correlated to the external world.

Such interpretation admits of a great deal of slippage. We have an effective instrument in our sensory system and we learn to use it. But, insists Helmholtz, its very 'imperfections' count against 'the idea of a pre-established harmony between the inner and the outer world' (1971, p. 240). Helmholtz's position is Darwinian:

> While the Darwinian theory treats exclusively of the gradual modification of a species after a succession of generations, we know that to a certain extent a single individual may adapt itself or become accustomed to circumstances under which it must live. . . Moreover, it is especially in the area of organic phenomena where purposiveness of structure has reached its highest form and excited the greatest admiration – the area of sense perception – that, as the latest developments in physiology teach us, this individual adaptation has come to play a most important role. (p. 240)

Evolution gives organisms structures that facilitate their successful engagement with nature; and the different species exhibit a greater or lesser degree of 'learning' in coming to cope with the environment. As these texts suggest, Helmholtz was committed to the notion of an active organism. He construed 'experience' as the 'trial and error' engagement of an active organism using its sensory machinery to acquire 'knowledge' of the external world.

Unconscious inferences

A second and related point of considerable contention is Helmholtz's notion of unconscious inferencing. It pointed the way to a research program in which the mechanisms of such inferencing would need to be theorized and experimentally demonstrated. Helmholtz was fully aware that referring to unconscious mechanisms as inference was bound to excite opposition since 'inference', then as now, suggests a *logical* process. 'Inference', he noted, was taken to be a capacity only of 'the highest conscious operations of the mind' (p. 217). Yet, he insisted, 'there appears to me in reality only a superficial difference between the inference of logicians and those inductive inferences whose results we recognize in the conceptions we gain of the outer world through our sensations' (p. 217). There is, however, one considerable difference – hardly 'superficial' – to accommodate: 'The chief difference is that the former inferences are capable of expression in words, while the latter are not' (p. 217). Still, according to Helmholtz, this difference does not justify the depreciation of *Kennen* as against *Wissen*. The Kantian restriction of judgment to inferences expressible in words and his failure to carry out the analysis of intuition into 'the elementary processes of thought' was, Helmholtz argued, an obstacle to an adequate under-standing of how we come to know. 'These judgments or inferences will, of course, remain unknown and inaccessible to philosophers as long as they inquire only into knowledge expressed in language' (1971, p. 391). Indeed!

Logicians' prejudices, shared by Kantian and British empiricist epistemologies, were but part of the problem Helmholtz had to face in advancing his idea of unconscious inferences. There were also positivist objections to postulating mechanisms purporting to 'lie behind' and explain phenomena. Turner points out that, by the 1880s, all hypo-thetical entities were being firmly rejected (Turner, 1982, pp. 160f.). Carl Stumpf, a student of Brentano, conceded that the term unconscious inference might be allowed if it were restricted to association. Apolo-gizing for Helmholtz's presumed carelessness, Stumpf suggested that Helmholtz need not have meant more than that. Of course, he did mean more than that, however difficult it might be to flesh out the idea without encouraging a more traditional metaphysics *à la* Kant or Fichte.

Helmholtz was also very much aware of the new understanding of modern science leading directly to what we now call positivism, and although he did not dismiss metaphyics, he shared with the scientists of his day a sense of the need to discriminate between 'science' and 'metaphysics'. It was, therefore, easy to read him incorrectly, then as now, as subscribing to a variant version of the dominant empiricist conception of science.

It must be admitted that Helmholtz lacked an articulated theory of mind. He was clearly not a Millian, and he rejected the Kant/Fichte notion of the transcendental ego. 'The Realist hypothesis is the simplest that can be formulated' (p. 385). On the other hand, what, for him, mind was is unclear. By the end of the century, mind and matter had rigidified as Cartesian substances. With good reason, Helmholtz seems to have found neither 'mind' nor 'matter' scientifically respectable. The latter, of course, was associated with the reductive materialism of Büchner and Dühring; the former bequeathed seemingly impossible problems for science. It is a matter of record that Helmholtz never addressed the issue posed in these terms. Mind/body, it seems, was, for Helmholtz, a pseudo-problem: of course, there are objects in the world and we do have experiences. Science needed to understand this causally – a task that required neither a transcendental ego nor Cartesian substances. As I argue in part II ('A limited program'), Helmholtz was surely correct in this, even if the conceptual questions remain unsolved.

Was Helmholtz's program too 'limited'?

Turner has suggested that, though plausible, 'obviously the new psychology could not accept such a limited program as Helmholtz's (Turner, 1982, p. 162). Turner's 'obviously' may betray his own sympathies. But those who wanted psychology to be a science of mind could not proceed empirically. For one thing (as no one noticed), a larger program would have required answers to questions that only Helmholtz's 'limited' program could provide. Indeed, a learning theory that assumes that learners already have meaningful perceptions simply assumes away the very fundamental problem of learning. Rooted in introspective theories, that approach simply dead-ended. Not surprisingly, psychology was thereupon redefined as the science of behavior. Having assumed that agents have meaningful experiences, it became easy to assume these away as irrelevant to psychology. People could then be treated as mindless and learning, defined as change in behavior. As Helmholtz and Wundt saw, another difficulty loomed: mind was social.

The role of Wundt

The revisionist picture of Wilhelm Wundt, the 'founder' of modern experimental psychology, has for some years been much favored. (See Danziger, 1979a, 1980b, 1980c; Leary, 1979; Rieber, 1980; Woodward 1982.) I do not intend to review that story, though I shall enter some demurrers. I concentrate on Wundt's role as regards the disciplinary definition of experimental psychology.

The phrase, 'physiological psychology', was not first used by Wundt. Moreover, Wundt seems to have benefited from Bain's *Senses and the Intellect* (1835) – the text that established the quaint precedent of beginning a systematic psychology with a chapter on the nervous system (Diamond,

1980). Wundt's own *Grundzüge der physiologischen Psychologie*, 1st edition, 1873, was a gigantic success. As Feldman remarked (in Rieber, 1980, p. 209), 'it was the first of the two achievements which marked the launching of psychology as an autonomous experimental discipline'; the other, of course, was the founding of Wundt's laboratory in Leipzig, in 1879.

No doubt the world was ready for Wundt, prepared by the remarkable current advances in physiology, neurology and psychophysics. Citing Ebbinghaus's 1908 comment, Diamond writes (in Rieber, 1980, p. 59) that 'Wundt was the first to graft all the nineteenth-century sproutings of the new psychology (sense physiology, personal equation, psychophysics, brain localization) onto the old, partially withered stock and thus to revivify it'. Wundt will still have two wars to fight, however: one, against the philosophers; the other, against the physiologists.

In America, William James heralded the *Grundzüge* with enthusiasm. So too did Sully, in England. Both saw 'the new psychology' as a physiological psychology. F. A. Lange, author of the famous *History of Materialism*, fastened on the following text:

> It is clear that the forebrain, in which the most significant functions of the cerebral cortex are concentrated, transforms sensory stimuli into extraordinarily complex movements of many forms. . . . Everything which we call Will and Intelligence resolves itself, as soon as it is traced back to its elementary physiological phenomena, into *nothing but* such transformations. (Wundt, *Grundzüge*, 1873, p. 228, quoted by Diamond with italics added, in Rieber, 1980, p. 62)

As Diamond says, what was 'admirable' in Wundt's presentation was 'his use of elementary physiological facts' as explanatory of *psychological* phenomena – since, for Lange, 'psychology was not limited to the study of consciousness' (1980, p. 62). Indeed, Wundt's book was seen to advance a project wholly in keeping with what Helmholtz and the psychophysicists and physiologists had been proposing: in Diamond's words, 'to find physiological foundations for all forms of mental activity'. Moreover, 'the term physiological psychology as used by him [i.e., Wundt] referred to just such use of physiological findings' (p. 63). Yet, as Diamond also points out, it was *just this* view of the matter which Wundt later characterized as '"widespread misunderstanding" about the nature of the new discipline' (Diamond, 1980).

What happened is clear enough. 'Physiological psychology' was 'experimental psychology', a term which Wundt had already used in his *Beiträge* of 1862. Moreover, an inquiry that was 'experimental' was surely 'scientific'. But need the 'experimental' be *physiological*? This was the link Wundt broke.

Diamond renders a valuable service by collating the changes in the opening pages of the five editions of Wundt's *Grundzüge*, from its publication in 1873 to the last edition of 1908–11. What we are helped to see thereby is the relation between physiology and psychology: moving from a straightforward physiological psychology to the delineation of experimental psychology as an autonomous science – entirely independent of physiology. To quote from one of the later editions:

> Of the two tasks that are . . . implied by the name of physiological psychology – one methodological, relating to the use of experiment, the other amplificatory, relating to the corporeal basis of mental life – it is the former that is more essential to psychology itself, while the latter has value chiefly with respect to the philosophic question about the overall unity of life processes. (Wundt, 1908/11, in Rieber, 1980, p. 169)

The reader should notice the hedged phrases, 'more essential' and 'chiefly', marking an ambiguity regarding what the non-philosophical relevance of physiology must be. The remark is characteristic of everything Wundt said thereafter, even if, today, many hold that Wundt thoroughly divorced psychology and physiology. (See Boring, 1929; Leary, 1979; Rieber, 1980.) Consider for instance, this unintelligible text from Wundt's 1897 *Outlines of Psychology*:

> The introduction of the experimental method into psychology was originally due to the modes of procedure in physiology. . . . For this reason experimental psychology is also commonly called 'physiological psychology'; and works treating it under this title regularly contain those supplementary facts from the physiology of the nervous system and the sense organs which require special discussion with a view to the interests of psychology, though in themselves they belong to physiology alone. (p. 24)

What, indeed, could these 'interests' be? How could they belong 'to physiology alone'? Is this the justification of the *pro forma* account of the central nervous system in today's psychology texts – introduced in every chapter 1 and then promptly ignored in the chapter devoted, say, to learning?

On the other hand, Wundt was crystal clear regarding the subject and tasks of psychology:

> The immediate contents of experience which constitute the subject-matter of psychology are under all circumstances processes of a complex character.

Accordingly,

> ... scientific investigation has three problems to be solved in succession. The *first* is the *analysis* of composite processes; the *second* is the *demonstration of the combinations* into which the elements discovered by analysis enter; the *third* is the *investigation of the laws* that are operative in the formation of such combinations. (Wundt, 1897, p. 25)

It can hardly be doubted that it was because of just this sort of programmatic claim, along with Wundt's assertion that 'introspection' – *inner Wahrnehmung*, not *Selbstbeobachtung* – was the 'foundation of psychology' (Danziger, 1979a, 1979b, 1980a, 1980b, 1980c), that Wundt came to be seen as the 'introspectionist' *par excellence and* a German *associationist*, who, having left physiology aside (with Mill), had also left German metaphysics and now, converging toward the 'truth', was moving in the direction of an empirical psychology in the British sense! Indeed, more generally, it seemed that empirical psychology – now, *experimental* psychology – had finally come into its own. It could now be admitted as one of the sciences – but only in the spirit in which the new positivist philosopher/physicists had recently defined science. To take this next step, we need to turn to Ernst Mach, philosopher, physicist and physiologist.

Mach's philosophy of science and his philosophy of psychology

Everyone knows that positivist philosophy of science came to dominate the conception of science at the end of the century. (See Passmore, 1966, ch. 14.) Leaving Helmholtz and Heinrich Hertz aside, a virtual tidal wave of variant positivisms was produced. Three of the distinct theses of late nineteenth-century positivism need to be sorted: first, the phenomenalist 'solution' to the materialism/idealism debate of nineteenth-century metaphysics – inspired as much by Kant as by the British empiricists; second, the Humean notion of causality; finally, a redefinition of the aims and goals of science – replacing the 'explanatory' by the 'descriptive'.

As is well-known, J. S. Mill had, in offering his definition of matter as 'the permanent possibility of sensation', produced a particularly influential version of positivism. A clear statement of this view – with some improvements – may be found in Mach's *Analysis of Sensations* (1883/1959). Here, matter is defined as 'a mental symbol standing for a relatively stable complex of sensational elements' (p. 363). The improvement over Mill was this:

> The world is not a mere sum of sensations. Indeed, I speak expressly of functional relations of the elements. But this conception not only makes Mill's 'possibilities' superfluous, but replaces them by something more solid, namely the mathematical conception of function. (Mach 1883/1959)

Mach, like Russell who will follow him, assumes a generalization of the Humean analysis of causality. Instead of the 'rigid' notion that 'a dose of effects follows upon a dose of cause', Mach offered the subtle conception of a mathematical function, by means of which we may display complicated relations 'according to what is required by the facts under consideration' (p. 89). Moreover, since 'bodies do not produce sensations [an incoherent idea for positivism] but complexes of elements (complexes of sensations) make up bodies', we may reject the illicit dichotomy between physical research and psychological research:

> The great gulf between physical research and psychological research persists only when we acquiesce in our habitual stereo-typed conceptions. A color is a physical object as soon as we consider its dependence, for instance on its luminous source, upon other colors, upon temperatures, upon spaces, and so forth. When we consider, however, its dependence upon the retina . . . it is a psychological object, a sensation. (p. 17)

Against both Kant *and* the realism of Helmholtz, then:

> For us, . . . the world does not consist of mysterious entities which by their interaction with another, equally mysterious entity, the ego, produce sensations, which alone are accessible. For us, colors, sounds, spaces, times, . . . are provisionally the ultimate elements, whose connection it is our business to investigate. (p. 29ff.)

This last sentence sets the tasks of science, establishing 'connections' between 'sensations', the 'compendious' or 'economical' arrangement of these. This involves, as a consequence, 'the elimination of all superfluous assumptions which cannot be controlled by experience, and above all, assumptions that are metaphysical in Kant's sense'. Accordingly, 'a whole series of troublesome pseudo-problems at once disappears' (p. 270).

The dualist question, 'How is it possible to explain feeling by the motion of the brain?' can never be answered, for 'the problem is not a problem' (p. 208). The world consists of 'elements' (sensations). If we 'neglect our own body' and merely consider those elements which make up 'foreign bodies', we are physicists. When we consider these in relation to our own body, we are in the domain of physiological psychology. Thus, its subject-matter is not different from that of physics and *this* science 'will unquestionably determine the relations the sensations bear to the physics of the body' (p. 210).

This was a remarkable performance, but its point and impact are still not well understood. Mach's defense of 'mathematical functions', mediated through Karl Pearson, was to have a great impact on subsequent philosophy of science and on quantitative methods in 'psychology'; but it is not usually acknowledged that Mach's conception of *psychology* anticipated *Carnap's*, that it was a thoroughgoing physiological view, and that, like J. B. Watson's, it was a physiological psychology without *minds*. But I am getting ahead of my story. We need first to consider the relation of this version of 'the new psychology' to Wundt's views.

'The new psychology': Wundt or Mach?

Like Mach, Wundt had argued that 'empirical psychology' cannot 'admit any fundamental difference between the methods of psychology and those of natural science' (Wundt, 1897, p. 9). This was innocent enough; but, like Mach, Wundt took it that, 'the question of the relation between psychical objects and physical objects disappears entirely' (p. 10). Here is the rest of the text, which sounds very much like Mach:

> The question of the relation between psychical and physical objects disappears entirely. They are not different objects at all, but one and the same content of experience, looked at in one case – in that of the natural sciences – after abstracting from the subject, in the other – in that of psychology – in their immediate character and complete relations to the subject. (Wundt, 1897, p. 10)

Yet this is exactly the *opposite* of Mach's conception, since Wundt begins from the point of view of the *subject* and, staying within experience, obliterates the distinction between 'inner experience' and 'outer experience'. Wundt, thus, is not far from Husserl or from James's 'Does consciousness Exist?' Wundt writes that 'every concrete experience immediately divides into two factors: into a content presented to us and our apprehension of this content' (p. 3ff.). The first of these we call 'objects of experience'; the second, 'the experiencing subject'. In turn, 'this division points to two directions in the treatment of experience'; that of the natural sciences, which 'concern themselves with the objects of experience, thought of as independent of the subject', and that of psychology, which investigates 'the whole content of experience' (p. 3). Natural science thus deals with 'mediated experience' and needs 'abstactions and hypothetical supplementary concepts' – atoms, molecules, and the like. Psychology deals with immediate experience and does not *need* these. For Wundt, then, psychology was not merely one of the sciences, it was the fundamental science. The step towards Husserl is clear enough.

But this phenomenalist-sounding (and somewhat phenomenological) treatment is not *positivist*. Wundt supposed that he could satisfy the critics of metaphysical psychology by insisting that his view needed no substantial mind, no *mind substance* – could proceed merely with the 'concept of the actuality of mind' (p. 314). Against Mach and the positivists, however, natural science *did* need *matter* as a 'fundamental supplementary concept'. Indeed a second such indispensable concept proved to be 'the causal activity of matter' (p. 311). *This*, however, had absolutely no bearing on psychology, for Wundt, since psychology employed the quite different and *directly knowable* phenomena of 'psychic causality'.

The central mechanism of 'psychic causality' was the Wundtian conception of apperception, a Leibnizian notion, central in Kant's doctrine and in Fichte's, but (as I have already remarked) nowhere to be found in the British tradition. Danziger's summary is convenient:

First, it expressed Wundt's dynamic standpoint, the attitude which caused him to characterize his own system as 'voluntaristic'. The basis of mental life was to be found not in the passive response to impression, nor in the reproductive play of associations, but in the activity of selective attention and discriminative judgement. He conceived of this activity as a real force, an 'aboriginal energy' which first expressed itself in impulsive movement. Second, the doctrine of apperception expressed the decidedly 'centralist' bias of Wundt as opposed to the 'peripheralism' of some of his contemporaries. (Danziger, 1979a, p. 216)

These ideas were simply buried by post-Wundtian, Machian psychology.

I have so far addressed only Wundt's vision of experimental psychology. I have omitted much that is pertinent, for instance Titchener's misunderstanding of Wundt's entire approach to 'introspection' and the distinction between Wundt and the behaviorists.

I have tried to establish two points regarding Wundt's role in the development of experimental psychology. First, Wundt contributed to the dead-ending of the Helmholtzian program for psychology. By disconnecting psychology from physiology – obscurely – Wundt also contributed to the influence of the Millian conception of psychology – with regard to the 'laws of the mind'. It was, of course, this version of 'experimental psychology' that the Americans finally rejected in favoring behaviorism. Secondly, Wundt was neither a phenomenalist nor a Humean, although, like so many others, he believed that metaphysics had no place in 'science'. The positivists of course read Wundt differently. His own central idea, that of an active and unitive mind capable of 'apperception', was itself attacked as metaphysical. The Machian alternative was *a phenomenalist physiological psychology – a psychology without a mind*.

Mind as social

There was at least one further problem, which Mill had tried to skirt, that interested Wundt: whether a psychology concerned with the discovery of the laws of mind could afford to ignore the social dimension of mental life. Wundt agreed with Helmholtz that *experimental* psychology had to limit its research program, because the study of the functioning of the 'higher mental faculties' would inevitably lead one to the irreducibly social. Wundt had distinguished two kinds of psychology, 'experimental' psychology and *Volkerpsychologie* – 'ethnic' or social psychology. There are, he wrote, 'certain facts at the disposal of psychology which, although they are not real objects, still have the character of relative permanence, and independence of the observer' (Wundt, 1897, p. 22). These facts are 'unapproachable by means of experiment in the common acceptance of the term', they are 'the mental products that have developed in the course of history, such as language, mythological ideas, and customs' (p. 23). They can be studied only historically as *Geisteswissenschaften*.

Neither Helmholtz nor Wundt was exactly clear about how to formulate the limits of their respective programs. David Leary has suggested that Wundt confined his program to the examination of 'the basic processes involved in the lower mental activities such as sensing, perceiving, feeling and willing' (Leary, 1979, p. 234). This suggests that 'cognition', a 'higher mental process', might have to be excluded altogether. For Helmholtz, however, the processes of unconscious inferencing were fully 'cognitive' and had to be predicated of animals. For Wundt, the matter is much less clear; for Helmholtz, but not for Wundt, brain physiology played the key role.

However this may be, Wundt's views on the limits of 'experimental' psychology, as well as his ideas on 'psychic causality', were buried by the Machians, in Germany, and, in America, by almost everybody. I say 'almost', here, because, as Danziger remarks, John Dewey and George Herbert Mead were much impressed by Wundtian arguments. The result was Chicago 'social psychology'.

I suggested earlier that Wundt had to fight two battles to define an autonomous psychology: one against the philosophers, the other against the physiologists. (See Leary, 1979.) Ironically, he won both, even if ultimately he lost the war. 'Psychology', once secured within the Academy, would, in America, be redefined as the science of behavior. Furthermore, Wundtian psychology, already under attack, would receive a knockout blow with the advent of World War I: more than anything else, the war convinced Americans that something was profoundly wrong with German social science.

The historical conjuncture which explains the redefinition of psychology

The phenomenal development of American industry in the last decades of the nineteenth century had direct consequences for academic psychology: it mobilized higher education in America, but especially graduate education, and it gave the exploding university new resources for addressing an enormous set of social problems that, up to that point, Americans had not yet become aware of.

Though the story is more complicated than I can sketch here, we must take account of the fact that in the course of less than 30 years, the Americans built a large university system, provisioned with PhD programs in psychology and the social sciences. Enrolments multiplied seven- and eight-fold. At the same time, problems of urbanization, poverty, class war, appeared almost all at once. In America, these were overlaid with racial implications and the effects of the most phenomenal immigration the modern world has known. When the 'social problem' hit America, it hit with a vengeance.

America, of course, has no feudal past or *ancien régime*. It was 'bourgeois' from its very beginnings. It only had the ideology of post-Reformation Enlightenment, and it lacked the idea of class. An 'anti-democratic' response to American problems would have been difficult to reconcile. The university was thoroughly middle class and its professoriat was not, as in Europe, a 'mandarin class' legitimated by tradition in a class-ridden society. In Europe, but not in America, the university could, at least until the catastrophe of World War I, conceive itself to be the guardian of national culture – of just those values requisite to reproduce the patrician class to which the professoriat supposed itself to belong.

But if America lacked tradition as a source of authority, it did not lack science (Bledstein, 1976, p. 326). The university spawned the opportunity to create a whole new set of roles – the professional of social problems, the 'social scientist' as technician (Danziger, 1979).

What did this mean for the American science of psychology? We need to look at the intellectual material available to American psychologists and see what of this could be used to secure for academic psychology a firm place in the universities of America. Once one asks the question, it is striking how widespread agreement on the answer is. Writing in 1929, Boring nearly says it all:

From about 1888 to 1895 a wave of laboratory-founding swept over America. . . . Americans were going to Germany, mostly to Wundt at Leipzig, and coming back filled with enthusiasm for making American psychology secure in experimentalism. Titchener and Münsterberg were imported in 1892. On the face of things, America was attempting to duplicate Germany; but under the surface, quite unrecognized at first, a psychology that resembled Galton's as much as Wundt's was being formed. Cattell, the senior after James, Ladd and Hall, had returned from Leipzig but little impressed with the importance of the generalized normal human adult mind and bent upon investigation of individual differences in human nature. Baldwin supported him. Finally, under the influence of John Dewey and pragmatism, the systematic structure of American psychology began to show. . . . American functionalism came into being, in bold relief against the Wundtian background which Titchener was there to provide. . . .

By 1900, the characteristics of American psychology were well defined: it inherited its physical body from German experimentalism, but got its mind from Darwin. American psychology was to deal with the mind in use. . . . Thorndike brought the animals into the formal laboratory . . . [and] then went over to the study of school children, and the mental tests increased. Hall helped here too with his pioneering in educational psychology. . . . Then Watson touched a match to the mass, there was an explosion, and behaviorism was left'. (Boring, 1929/1950, pp. 493ff.)

Galton, the half-cousin of Darwin, was, of course, the first to apply the normal law of error to the measurement of mental ability; he developed the 'index of co-relation' – r – which was brought to its present form by Karl Pearson, the British trumpet for the philosophy of Ernst Mach. Galton, a racist, had spent much of his life working on the problem of *mental* inheritance. He was not, to be sure, himself a 'psychologist' in the then-current sense of the term.

E. L. Thorndike did bring the animals 'into the laboratory', but his animal psychology was *not* inspired by Helmholtzian interests in the mechanisms of 'unconscious inferencing'. It was inspired rather by a conviction, as Boring puts it, that 'animals show in their learning no evidence of inferential reasoning or what we should nowadays call "insight", but learn simply by the chance formations of associations in their random experience' (Boring, 1929/1950, p. 555)! Even Titchener, alone in promoting 'the generalized normal human adult mind' and not 'minds in use', offered a Millian version of Wundt and a Machian version of 'apperception'. Cattell, Baldwin and Walter McDougall (who, in 1908, had written the first textbook that defined psychology as 'the science of behavior') were, like all the rest of America's experimental psychologists, interested only in the 'mind in use'. Which is to say: they were interested in *behavior*.

Watson's 1913 programmatic statement was of course aimed against 'introspective psychology' and toward securing a truly scientific psychology. Watson was aided and abetted in this by the total European victory of Mach's version of the positivist theory of science – including somewhat more vaguely his version of physiological psychology. There were other more direct influences on Watson, but that is hardly the point. Watson played the part of 'touching a match to the mass'. Nothing he said was actually new, not even the idea that scientific psychology's 'theoretical goal is the prediction and control of behavior' (Watson, 1913/1963, p. 158). But he surely identified the straws in the wind alright, however oddly. In the same paper, he feels encouraged to think his position 'defensible', since

> Those branches of psychology which have already partially withdrawn from the parent, experimental psychology, and which are consequently less dependent upon introspection are today in the most flourishing condition. Experimental pedagogy, the psychology of drugs, the psychology of advertising, legal psychology, the psychology of tests and psychopathology are all vigorous growths. (p. 158)

The classic case of the tail wagging the dog!

Still it mattered far less that behaviorism sought to expunge 'introspection' than that it promoted the notion that 'experimental psychology' should model itself on 'applied psychology' and that the *theoretical* goal of scientific psychology itself was simply the *prediction and control of behavior*: 'positivism has [always] been the favorite philosophy for those who wished to justify science in terms of its usefulness for achieving established social goals' (Danziger, 1979a, p. 225). Positivism alone, it's true, did not father the American definition of scientific psychology. That definition, by the way, is now quite native to the speech and thinking even of those psychologists who are not applied psychologists and who are in no way committed to either behaviorism or positivism. It is not clear what it would take to rid psychology of its historically produced misconception of itself. My own effort, here, has been to identify the 'accidents' that have brought psychology to its present form – that large amalgam of philosophical and institutional factors that has led us to the prevalent notion of an autonomous scientific psychology. I want now to proceed more straightforwardly to argue, in effect, that Helmholtz's alternative remains a viable and instructive alternative.

A limited program

Introduction

Perhaps 10,000 of the more than 60,000 accredited psychologists in the English-speaking world do what might be called basic research in psychology. The others have a primary interest in the applications to specific areas, which often itself involves research. Thus, educational psychology defines a subdiscipline, 'theoretical' as well as 'applied'. Most of the 60,000, however, would probably agree that their interest lies in 'behavior'.

I want to argue, here, that there is a program currently involving a minority of researchers, that addresses basic psychological research and defines psychology as an autonomous science, neither a social science nor a biological science. I argue, further, that this effort, the program of neuropsychology, cannot explain behavior, but *can* provide an understanding of the psychological mechanisms which ground our human powers and human competences. The program is difficult, also important and distinctly limited in scope. It will never be the central concern of most people who are drawn to 'psychology', and this may be as it should be. I want also to argue, however, that any inquiry interested in explaining, predicting, and controlling behavior is inevitably multi-disciplinary – because behavior is itself a complex product of a number of co-operating systems. I begin with this idea.

Stratification

Speaking of a human being from the point of view of biology (including biochemistry), we can think of an organism as an ordered complex of orderly complex systems. Roughly, biochemistry begins at the level of atoms and molecules and works 'upward' through larger and more complex molecules to those systems we normally identify as biological – organelles, cells, tissues, organs and, ultimately, the molar organism itself. (The metaphor of 'levels' is a great convenience.) One biologist may be concerned with the interrelations of gross anatomical features, where particular organs, the nervous system and the like, form constituents of an interacting system. Another may be concerned with cells and his analysis may be indifferent to species differentiation or even to the macrosystems that hierarchies of particular cells constitute. Still another may treat an entire ecosystem as the pertinent object of inquiry. As David Hull says, these levels are not 'givens', but emerge as inquiry proceeds and, as he perceptively remarks, 'no one really questions the fact that all these phenonomena are part of one and the same reality.' Yet, he continues, it is one thing to recognize this fact and quite another to construct scientific theories that reflect this presumed unity' (Hull, 1974, p. 31). No scientific theory talks about everything in all its detail, and all scientific theories embed an ontology: they tell us what the world 'contains', atoms and molecules, cells and mammals. But they need not and generally do not tell us how these 'parts' are related – to one another or to the 'whole' of reality. That is, the abstractive interrogation which propels modern science proceeds so unevenly that, though we have many theories about the different 'parts' of reality, we are hardly clear how to integrate them all so as to reflect the 'unities' of naive experience or of large scientific theories. As Hull observes: 'considerable contingency exists between the phenomena at various levels as they are now analyzed – and in some cases the analyses are even incompatible' (p. 134). Thus, although each such analysis may give an account of processes essential to the functioning of the organism, *individually*, each has an *impoverished* view of the whole (Wimsatt, 1976). Organisms are extremely complicated complexes. Hence, although theory demands that we think in terms of system closures isolability, and the like, it is almost certain that an enormous number of extra-systemic causal transactions are continually taking place – which are themselves correspondingly complex. (See Weiss, 1971; Grobstein, 1976.)

Moreover, although it is convenient to speak of the 'building blocks' of life, the metaphor is misleading whenever it leads us to imagine that 'whole/part' relations are simply additive or conjunctive. On such a view, hierarchies can be 'decomposed' as Wimsatt says, 'in a nestable manner'. This assumes that we can individuate and map the existing systems – but we cannot at present do this. We must also then assume, against the evidence, that inter-level connections are irrelevant to what happens intra-level, that the presence of sub- and supra-systems is not causally pertinent (Wimsatt, 1976, Schaffner, 1976).

Here, we look at things bottom-up. Activities and processes occurring at any 'level' may have as outcomes of their causal transactions, phenomena at some next higher level, the properties of which are not predicable of the structures of thus-generating lower levels. These in turn become causally efficacious in transactions at their level and at the next higher level, and so on upward in the system. For example, proteins are capable of at least eight major activities of which the amino acids from which they are polymerized are not capable. Moreover, complete information about the atomic positions an unknown protein may occupy does not enable us to infer even that that protein is, for example, an enzyme, still less what its specific causal properties are. Cells have properties of different kinds from those that protein molecules exhibit; so, too, brains have different properties from those of any of their 'components'.

Looking at matters top-down, some higher-level processes appear to penetrate in a causal way at lower levels. This frequently overlooked complication has been explored by a number of biologically oriented theorists: Michael Polanyi (1968), P. A. Medawar (1974), H. H. Pattee (1972, 1973, 1974, 1976), and with special reference to psychological activities, Paul Weiss (1971), Karl Pribram (1976, 1977, 1982), Carol Fowler and Michael Turvey (1982), and others. Thus, even at the most elementary levels, for instance at the level of the action of the DNA molecule, there are higher principles of potential control over lower-order regularities, 'ruling', as it were, such finer-grained operations and processes from above. The clearest examples concern the coordinated movements of organisms that are intelligible primarily in terms of survival value. There, as Fowler and Turvey write, one is drawn to a 'grammar of restrictions' on physiological functioning itself. Indeed, Pribram has offered considerable evidence favoring the hypothesis that 'acts' – not mere movements – are represented in the cerebral cortex.

Sometimes, as the foregoing suggests, the configurational properties which are realized are those which our naive experience singles out as 'fundamental'. These, at least, insure the pertinence of the objective distinctions between the living and the non-living, the minded and the non-minded. Life and mind, however, are activities just as are gravity and magnetism – even if, viewed in accord with *our interests*, there remain enormous differences between the activities, the 'functional properties', the causal powers of the inorganic and the living, and between the minded and the unminded. But, the picture is still incomplete. Persons are surely minded, but they are also culturally emergent in the sense that they have distinctive capacities (actual properties) – for instance, linguistic abilities – predicable of them only in virtue of the causal outcomes of their developing biologically within a peculiarly complex social environment.

These considerations are not intended as such as refutations of vitalism or Cartesianism. Those theories are provisionally rescued by postulating different fundamental substances as necessary to the different activities acknowledged. But they do suggest the extravagance of such speculations: there is no need to postulate a *vis viva* or a *res cogitans*.

There is however no reductionism intended here. I take it that no one denies that the CNS is the basis ('infrastructure') of psychological phenomena. The more interesting question remaining is whether neural and biochemical proceses can explain the emergent psychological and social activities that we concede to be actual. And that question is itself ambiguous: focusing now on the reality of these phenomena, now on the complexity of the conditions of their explanation. We are invited to choose between a 'stratified' and a 'reductive' monism.

It is quite clear that biochemical studies of the life processes are not as such committed to a reductive materialism. No biologist denies the reality of emergent life processes. What of psychology? Roy Bhasker offers an ingenious argument to expose the bizarre comclusions that result from applying reductive materialism to psychology.

Thus, suppose B says to A, 'Pass the salt' and A does so. Call this action X_a. Then, either (1) X_a is the unique causal consequence of neurophysiological states N1, N2 . . . Nn such that X_a would have been performed without B's speech action, or (2) B's speech action is a causal element in bringing about X_a. (1), reductionism, implies

> A form of Leibnizian pre-established harmony of monads, in which each person's neurophysiology is so synchronized with every other's that it appears as if they were talking and laughing, smiling and winking. And in which each persons's neurophysiology is so synchronized with the nature of every other object that it appears as if they were fitting and turning; digging and building. (Bhaskar, 1979, p. 135ff.)

On (2), since the relation between A and B would involve more than a physical relation, would (let us say) be *hermeneutic* between A and B, the psychological states of A and B would be irreducible and yet also real and causally efficacious. In a word, neurophysiological closure is broken whenever a person, responding to a sudden shower, opens an umbrella to keep from getting wet and whenever an animal takes evasive action! To cling to reductive materialism under these circumstances is to opt for some form of universal system closure – Laplacean determinism, for instance.

Realism and psychology

The foregoing is meant as a key to the refutation of reductive materialism and the defense of a 'stratified' monism. Ontic dualism is not yet refuted, since one might always deny stratification (within a monism) and hold instead that physical and mental powers must, disjunctively, be assigned to different substrates. Classically, this returns us to the famous Cartesian problem of causal interaction: How does mind substance causally affect matter? But emergent powers of complex physical configurations are already admitted at the biological level. Stratification and inter-level causality are features of the world apart from the psychological. If so, then much of the motivation for ontic dualism disappears. There is then a close connection between a full-fledged realist theory of science, a rejection of 'ontic dualism' and an affirmation of what may be called 'attribute pluralism' – that is, the view that material things are 'capable of exhibiting qualities, properties and relations that cannot, in principle, be characterized in purely physical terms' (Margolis, 1984, p. 10). The implications for the philosophy of psychology are plain. Even if we rejected reductive materialism, we can reconcile admitting 'psychological' activities with materialism without subscribing in any way to the reductive strategies of materialism, behaviorism, the 'identity theory', 'eliminative materialism' or the like. We can do so, consistently with acknowledging psychological phenomena to be as intentionally complex as may have to be admitted – without contesting their reality or irreducibility.

Realism pertinently implies:

1   A given system has physical properties, includes such and such components, is structured in such and such a way (for instance, the atomic structure of molecules).
2   Its activities (its causal capabilities) need not be able to be described solely in terms of (1) (for example, enzymes).
3   It has whatever causal powers it has in virtue at least of (1).
4   Its properties at the level of functioning as a system may causally affect its component processes.

Point (3) discriminates between the realism here favored and ontic dualism; and it facilitates opposing those forms of cognitive psychology that develop only functional, abstract theories of cognitive states and processes, as in AI and so-called 'intentional psychology' (Kitchner, 1984). It accommodates a neuropsychology concerned with specifying actual biochemical mechanisms, which, perhaps in a piecemeal fashion, contribute to the evolution of intentionally characterized psychological activities. A heuristic reading of functional properties is entirely neutral regarding ontic dualism, it permits psychological inquiry to proceed somewhat independently of biology. On the realist view psychology *cannot* genuinely be pursued apart from biology, since, as incarnate, those psychological properties are construed as outcomes of their biological structures. (4) at least permits us to acknowledge that, as in control systems theory, 'feedback' plays a key role in system functioning (Dewan, 1976), that the system properties of the molecule 'constrain' nuclear forces in chemical transactions, that at some emergent level 'conscious properties are seen to supersede the more elemental physiochemical forces' (Sperry 1969).

This view is hardly novel but, until recently, it has been largely the neuroscientists who have tried to clarify it. R. W. Sperry remarked in

1965 that 'one had to search a long way in philosophy and especially in science' for evidence of the view that 'mental forces or events are capable of causing physical changes in an organism's behavior or its neurophysiology' – *without* implications of dualism (Sperry, 1976, p. 165). It was often wrongly supposed that if the functionally specified properties of a system were causal, they had to be suitably reduced. A thoroughly realist interpretation, however, admits interlevel causal complexities. Variants of the general thesis have for some time been championed in Pribram's 'structural pragmatism' (1965) – renamed 'constructional realism' (1976) – and in W. B. Weimer's strenuously defended 'structural realism' (1976). Donald Campbell, however misled by Popper, was surely on the right track (1974); and more recently, William Wimsatt (1976a, 1976b) and Roy Bhaskar (1979) have given sophisticated arguments in favor of the view.

Most psychologists, I suspect, would not hold that neurophysiology was independent of psychology. Still, much experimental psychology, particularly recent cognitive psychology, betrays such a penchant. Karl Pribram is surely justified in having observed that his own proposals are 'repeatedly and universally quoted when they appear devoid of their neurological skin, flesh, and bones', but are 'totally ignored when instantiated and substantiated [as in his] *Languages of the Brain*' (Pribram, 1971, p. 361ff.). Both current practice in experimental psychology and the plausibility (as Pribram put it) that psychology must 'build on its own level without recourse to physiology' are due largely to the historical contingencies I have already sketched in Part I. Behaviorism became the Machian form of instrumentalism, in psychhology; and realist explanations were expunged. Experimental psychology of the sort published in *The Journal of Experimental Psychology, Learning, Memory and Cognition*, is characteristically Wundtian – in the pre-Titchnerian sense! – and shares a taste for anti-realism. Discrimination, reaction studies, and the like are aimed at testing functional hypotheses with no regard to physiological mechanisms. The assumption is frequently made that busy psychologists cannot and need not wait for the results of current neuroscience. So-called 'intentional psychology', though characteristically Millian, now has the advantage of computer technologies and mathematical and logical modelling techniques unavailable to Mill. A machine 'simulation' now explains psychological phenomena by producing an 'equivalent output' – the AI version of the behaviorist dictum that two organisms are in the same psychological state when their behaviors or behavioral dispositions are identical.

Before I say more about the limited – Helmholtzian-like – program of neuropsychology, mentioned earlier, I must broach another issue, that of the relation of the social sciences to psychology. What has thus far been urged can be summarized by affirming that neuropsychology may well be autonomous in that it is not merely a subdiscipline of biology or neurophysiology. The question remains whether psychology is autonomous with respect to sociology.

Psychology and the social sciences

The question divides into two. First, can methodological individualism be sustained, and second, assuming that the answer to this question is no, can we, for purposes of psychological inquiry, distinguish between the social and the infrapsychological dimensions of the mental life of persons?

Methodological individualism has been variously characterized and much discussed. I cannot here review the literature, or hope to convince the unconvinced. The issue, however, is essential to the question of an autonomous psychology. As Bhaskar defines it, 'methodological individualism is the doctrine that facts about societies, and social phenomena generally, are to be explained solely in terms of facts about individuals' (Bhaskar, 1979, p. 34). He also insists rightly that when we consider those properties that are uniquely characteristic of persons, 'the real problem appears to be . . . how one could ever give a nonsocial (that is strictly individualistic) explanation of individual, at least cha-racteristically human, behavior!' (p. 35). Explanation here, must, however detailed, appeal to irreducible social predicates.

Consider only that language is the paradigmal socially structured human activity, real only as incarnate in the practices of individuals; but pre-existing for a given cohort and functioning as the very medium of their speech-acts. Language cannot be analysed in terms of those aggregated acts themselves. The point has been made from a variety of quarters: as in Saussure's thesis that only an entire society can 'possess' a language and then only in the sense that 'theorists idealize from time to time the structure that actual discourse may be thought to approximate' (Margolis, 1984, p. 80), and in cognate claims similar to Marxism, to hermeneutics, and Wittgensteinian theory. Barry Barnes and David Bloor, writing from the latter perspective argue:

Concept application is not a social activity in the sense that it is determined by a culturally given classification of reality, but a social activity which gives rise to and develops the pattern of that very classification. The pattern does not account for the activity; rather the activity accounts for the pattern. (Barnes, 1981, p. 310; see, Manicas and Rosenberg, 1985)

But if so, then, if psychological phenomena are modelled linguistically, and if language is non-reducibly social, then psychology cannot be altogether independent of sociology. It would seem to belong to 'the same system of "human studies" of which sociology and anthropology form distinct parts' (Margolis, 1984, p. 68). Was Comte (above, Part I) correct, then? Is there no science between physiology and social science?

Comte is wrong. There is such a science. I must now identify what remains for an autonomous psychology when we *exclude* the irreducibly social. It was just this that was earlier referred to as the infrapsychological. The answer is linked to denying that the essential aim of psychology is to explain *behavior*. It is the proper aim of psychology to explain the distinctly human capacities we exhibit in growing up and conducting our lives in the real world. The 'infrapsychological', then, refers to the causal mechanisms of perception, cognition memory, motivation and the like, at least partly innate biologically, presupposed in the process by which a human becomes a member of some particular human society (Manicas and Secord, 1983).

There is, evidently, a biological component which 'determines' the infrapsychological. Yet, all realized human capacities – the capacity to think, to perceive and to feel – are realized *only* in a fully-social environment. Given, then, that their realization is epigenetic, we cannot actually separate the biological from the social component in any additive way (Manicas, 1983). Nevertheless, just as the non-social 'environment' can affect how and whether genetically determined human potentialities are ever realized, the social 'environment' has a similar influence. This means that Lévy-Bruhl's question, 'Do they think like us?' is entirely meaningful. It may not even be a question merely of beliefs and assumptions; there is always the possibility that neurological mechanisms are themselves alterable: as a consequence of different social environment (Blakemore and Cooper, 1970).

It is, then, an empirical question. Anthropology, comparative physiology, comparative psychology are bound to play their role. We cannot say in advance whether there are such socially induced variants or whether those there are are significant (Manicas, 1983), but we may reasonably assume what Barnes calls a shared 'natural rationality'; consequently, a 'tolerant theory'. Encountered differences in modes of thought or the like should be construed as cultural differences and no more than that. The same (or substantially similar) psychological capacities, which define human nature, appear to issue in different culturally structured modes (Barnes, 1976). Also, since we actually know so little about even the most elementary psychological capacities, and since, as I would argue, there is still so much to learn from the study of the hominids and pre-hominids, we can hardly escape the assumption.

Our ignorance is not due to the 'youth' of the science; it is due more to the particular factors that have largely determined the development of scientific 'psychology', the philosophical and institutional factors mentioned in Part I. We are perhaps only now at the point at which we can undo the damage of the preposterous idea that a scientific psychology has as its primary task 'the explanation and control of behavior'. Given the genotypic uniqueness of humans, their epigenetic development, the way in which their realized competences (even emotions) are social constructions of such genetic and epigenetic materials, the social complexity of human action itself, it would be incredible if any science, especially a psychological science, could be expected to improve on what appears to be a very keenly developed natural explanatory ability (Manicas, 1982).

Problems in cognitive psychology

Walter Weimer has rightly remarked that 'explicating the nature of concept formation is perhaps the most important task faced by psychology' (Weimer, 1975, p. 648). The task is not addressed solely to language. All learning, all memory, all action appears to require some ability to classify particulars as instances of abstract categories or kinds. This is the problem of tacit knowledge or, in Gestalt terms, the problem of the 'Höffding principle'. Philosophers speak of it as the problem of abstraction. AI theorists label it the problem of 'character recognition'. But most of what is known about it is radically incomplete – and much that we claim to know is simply untenable.

I turn to a recent account by David Kelly and Janet Kreuger (1984). Kelly and Kreuger argue that the 'classical paradigm' for experiments on concept-formation were largely irrelevant, for, as Jerome Bruner notes, they examine 'conceptual attainment with the perceptual-abstraction phase bypassed' (p. 44). Classical theories, which feature the logical notions of intension and extension and more recent 'cluster' and 'prototype' theories, either presuppose genuine abstraction at some stage in their argument or render it a total mystery. In addition to the genuinely intractable local problems of current theories, the philosopher's standard query regarding the very idea of abstraction continues to have force: 'The observation that two objects are similar, . . . will involve at least the concept SIMILARITY, which is just as abstract as any contents which abstraction is supposed to explain' (p. 63ff.). We have hardly budged from Meno's paradox (Weimer, 1973).

As Weimer suggests (1975, p. 278), the mechanism of abstraction can be neither 'subtractive' nor 'associative'. But if so, we have two choices: either to adopt some sort of innatist theory, *à la* Plato, or to hold, with Weimer, that 'all concept formation is creative or productive' (p. 278). The first option is most clearly advanced by Fodor:

> If learning a language is literally a matter of making and confirming hypotheses about the truth conditions associated with predicates, then [it] presupposes the ability to use expressions coextensive with each of the elementary predicates of the language being learned.
>
> But the truth conditions associated with any predicate L [of some natural language] can be expressed in terms of the truth conditions associated with the elementary predicates of L. [Hence] one can learn what the semantic properties of a term are only if one already knows the language [i.e., a language not learned naturally] which contains a term having the same semantic properties. (This is conveniently quoted from Margolis, 1984, p. 79.)

As Fodor himself makes clear, the theory entails that it is impossible to learn a genuinely new concept: 'One can't learn [that is, acquire by a cognitive process] a conceptual system richer than the conceptual system that one starts with, where learning is a process of hypothesis formation and confirmation.' This is, *prima facie*, a startling enough conclusion: it should, I suggest, force us to examine its presuppositions. For one thing, the meanings of words and sentences are not explained in social terms, but depend upon some sort of verificationism and Platonism. For another, Fodor assumes along with his 'empiricist' opponents (the 'abstractionists' and associationists), that 'the only relations between contents of cognitive states which make a process involving those states a cognitive process are the sorts of logical functions used in classical experiments. *Logical functions hold between abstract predicates*' (Kelly and Kreuger, 1984, p. 64, my emphasis).

There is indeed a relation between 'learning' and the 'inductive model' of science. But Fodor's assumptions construe it backwards. Certainly, the idea of a distinct inductive logic has wrought considerable damage (Goodman, 1955). Also, as Weimer remarks, 'we should cease talking about science "learning by induction" and try to understand how the mind constructs its knowledge from its (tremendously impoverished) input' (Weimer, 2975, p. 474; see also Hesse, 1974; Sober 1978). More crudely put, Hume was not in error in relegating nondemonstrative inference to 'animal belief'. We would then be nearer to the truth if we modelled 'scientific method' not on 'logic' but on 'animal belief'.

We need to flesh the theme out a little. One way of doing so – fully in the spirit, if not the letter of Helmholtz – would have us consider the possibility that:

> abstraction is a preconceptual process, involving nonpropositional modes of cognition such as perception. It would not be a rational process, strictly speaking, since there are no logical relations, strictly speaking, among non-propositional contents. (Kelly and Kreuger, 1984, p. 93)

Kelly and Kreuger rightly insist that abstraction is a cognitive process, but they manage to escape the logician's conception of 'inference' and the philosopher's conception of 'cognitive' – where these are restricted to logical relations among propositions. Moreover, Kelly and Kreuger imply as well the rejection of 'information processing' models of *perception, a fortiori*, information processing models of cognition. This means at least that the early and influential theoretical work of Ulric Neisser, Ralph Norman Haber, Lachman and Lachman, Sperling, Sternberg and others needs to be rejected or radically revised. Neisser and Haber have changed their minds, strong evidence in itself of the demise of a research program (Neisser, 1976; Haber, 1983). Of course, it hardly ushers in a successful alternative, but it does afford a clue.

One thing that seems plain is the revived pertinence of animal learning, not, of course, as the behaviorist sees it, but as Weimer, Campbell, Pribram and Kandell have seen it. As Weimer says,

> the problems of nondemonstrative inference are the problems of understanding how the nervous system, from its preconscious determination of the orders of sensory experience to the higher mental processes such as human thought, attempts to model, with ever increasing degrees of adequacy, the environment that the organism confronts. There is no difference in kind between the scientist inferring the most esoteric theory of reality on the one

hand, and the simplest organism's inferring the presence of food or danger in its environment. (Weimer, 1975, p. 455)

There is no difference in kind in the sense that both capacities are creative and productive. There is an enormous difference in kinds of capacities and in content. Human thought is surely linked to language (and complicated by it). But the psychologist's task is understanding the general mechanism that give us *and* other organisms our immense, if qualitatively different, cognitive powers. There is, therefore, no reason to restrict inquiry to human concept formation alone. This much at least is neutral as between Chomsky and his critics. (See Margolis, 1984, pp. 82ff.)

Intentionality and animal intelligence

It may be thought that the foregoing is inconsistent with the idea that psychological states are inherently intentional and that, accordingly, they are best modelled on the propositional character of language. Three points may be pressed. First, because we identify and characterize psychological states thus, it does not follow that all the mechanisms that produce them are intentional or homuncular (Dennett, 1983). Second, insofar as we must identify psychological states thus (even assuming that we must do so), it remains true, as Margolis argues, that animal psychology cannot fail to be anthropomorphized. In this sense, our cognitive ascriptions to animals are heuristic in form, even when they are realistically intended. Third, there is an enormous difference, easily missed, between holding that intentional states may be best characterized in terms of a linguistic model and holding that, as Patricia Smith Churchland has put it, 'where there is cognition, there is also linguistic representation, no matter how far, phylogenetically or ontogenetically, the creature is from overt language' (1980, p. 189). The first view is noncommittal on the nature of 'representation'; the second holds that, in effect, all cognition satisfies the constraints of a sentential automaton in accord with which its 'processing' can be 'described in terms of the semantic and syntactic relations among . . . content-specifying sentences' (1980, p. 188). On this view 'to give an intentional description to an organism is to ascribe the concept of the embedded property or properties to the organism' (Turvey et al., 1981, p. 285).

However, not only is information processing not to be confused with information exchange (Churchland, 1980, p. 190) but information processing itself may well 'consist of transformations that bear no relation to those of deductive or inductive logic, e.g., amplification, filtering, averaging, integrating, etc. 'This is not the place to advocate particular theories of the processes involved in ecological transactions between organism and environment except perhaps to remark that no one thinks that the question is child's play (Churchland, 1980, p. 197). Nevertheless, once we abandon the fantastic program that pretends there is some sort of univocal invariance between ('stimulus' and 'response', or that 'information' comes prepacked for use by a sentential automaton – both notions very much favored by those who believe psychology is primarily meant to explain behavior – we can guess the intended pertinence of papers with such titles as 'Command Neurons in Pleurobranchaea Receive Synaptic Feedback from the Motor Network They Excite.' (The example is Churchland's.) Surely, such inquiry will not give us the whole story but who every supposed that it would? Churchland writes:

A neurophysiological account of how an organism processes information will include hypotheses about what really is the information contained in certain neuronal states at various levels from the periphery, what information is filtered in and filtered out, and how information is integrated. . . . The increase in complexity in the nervous system as one moves up the phylogenetic scale is admittedly breathtaking, but there is no reason to suppose that the increased complexity is anything more than increased complexity or to suppose that representing is an emergent property absolutely inexplicable in terms of the underlying physical structure. (1980, p. 197)

But we must not be misled. Churchland would not deny, I take it, that increased complexity is not just increased complexity, in the sense of hierarchically successive higher levels of the organisation of lower level elements. These elements are, as she rightly says, not 'absolutely inexplicable'. Our ability to give a causal account of emergent biological functions in terms of biochemistry – our ability even to synthesize life processes from the non-living – hardly eliminates the explanatory complexity of those functions, beyond the resources of the biochemical vocabulary.

Experimental psychology and the social-psychological sciences

I do not, however, wish to leave the closing impression that I take all 'psychological' inquiry that is not neuropsychological to be wrong or useless. I do insist that physiology is absolutely indispensable to experimental psychology. But there is also all that 'psychology' that, on the present view, is appropriately part of what Margolis calls 'the human studies'. Noteworthy here is the older work of John Dewey, in *Human Nature and Conduct*, much of Freud's work, as well as the recent work of such authors as Paul Secord and Rom Harré.

There is also the entire range of what is usually called 'applied psychology' – educational, industrial psychology, and the like. On the present argument, these are also part of 'the human studies' (the social and psychological sciences). Here I confess some unease. The same history that explains why experimental psychology took the wrong direction also served (the reader will recall) to explain the present emphasis in 'psychology' on 'applied' psychology. Nevertheless, there can be little doubt that current 'psychology' has very much overlooked the overwhelming presence of the social. This evidence is everywhere. But for our present purpose, we may close this account, having brought psychology back and forward to both the neurophysiological and the social.

REFERENCES

Where two dates are given after an author's name (for example, Boring, E. G. 1929/1950), the first indicates the year of original publication and the second the edition referred to in the text whose publication details are cited here.

Ayala, F. and Dobzhansky, T. (eds) 1974: *The Problem of Reduction in Biology*. Berkeley, Cal.: University of California Press.
Barnes, B. 1981: On the conventional character of knowledge and cognition. *Philosophy of Social Sciences*, 11, 303–33.
Bhaskar, R. 1979: *The Possibility of Naturalism: a philosophical critique of the contemporary human sciences*. Brighton, Sussex: Harvester Press.
Blakemore, C. and Cooper, G. F. 1970: Development of the brain depends upon the visual environment. *Nature*, 228.
Bledstein, B. 1976: *The Culture of Professionalism: the middle class and the development of higher education in America*. New York: W. W. Norton.
Boas, G. 1924: *French Philosophies of the Romantic Period*. Baltimore: Johns Hopkins University Press.
Boring, E. G. 1929/1950: *A History of Experimental Psychology*. New York: Appleton-Century-Crofts.
Campbell, D. 1974: Downwards causation in hierarchically organized biological systems. In Ayala and Dobzhansky, 1974, 179–86.

Churchland, P. S. 1980: A Perspective on Mind & Brain Research. *The Journal of Philosophy*, LXXVII (4), 185–207.

Danziger, K. 1979a: The positivist repudiation of Wundt. *Journal of the History of the Behavioral Sciences*, 15, 205–30.

Danziger, K. 1979b: The social origins of modern psychology: positivist sociology and positivist sociology of knowledge. In A. R. Buss (ed.), *The Social Context of Psychological Theory*, New York: Irvington, 27–45.

Danziger, K. 1980a: The history of introspection reconsidered. *Journal of the History of the Behavioral Sciences*, 16, 241–62.

Danziger, K. 1980b: Wundt and the two traditions in psychology. In Reiber, 1980, 73–87.

Danziger, K. 1980c: Wundt's theory of behavior and volition. in Reiber, 1980, 89–115.

Danziger, K. 1982: Mid-nineteenth century British psycho-physiology: a neglected chapter in the history of psychology. In Woodward and Ash, 1982, 119–46.

Dennett, D. C. 1983: Intentional systems of cognitive ethology: 'The Panglossian Paradigm' defended. *Behavioral and Brain Sciences*, 6, 343–90.

Dewan, E. M. 1976: Consciousness as an emergent causal agent in the context of control system theory. In Globus et al., 1976, 171–98.

Diamond, S. 1980: Wundt before Leipzig. In Reiber, 1980, 3–70.

Fodor, J. A. 1968: *Psychological Explanation*. New York: Random House.

Fodor, J. A. 1975: *The Language of Thought*. New York: Crowell.

Fowler, C. A. and Turvey, M. T. 1982 Observational perspective and descriptive level in perceiving and acting. In Weimer and Palermo, 1982, vol. 2, 1–19.

Globus, G. G., Maxwell, G. and Savodnik, I. (eds) 1976: *Consciousness and the Brain: a scientific and philosophical inquiry*. New York: Plenum Press.

Goodman, N. 1955: *Fact, Fiction and Forecast*. London: Athlone.

Grene, M. and Mendelsohn, E. 1976: *Topics in the Philosophy of Biology*. Dordrecht, Holland: Reidel, vol. XXVII, Boston Studies in the Philosophy of Science.

Grobstein, C. 1976: Organizational levels and explanation. In Grene and Mendelsohn, 1976, 145–52.

Haber, R. N. 1983: The impending demise of the icon: a critique of the concept of iconic storage in visual information processing. *Behavioral and Brain Sciences*, 6, 1–54.

Helmholtz, H. 1971: *Selected Writings*. Edited, with an Introduction by Russell Kahl. Middleton, Conn: Wesleyan University Press. See especially: The Relation of the Natural Sciences to Science in General (1852), Recent Progress in the Theory of Vision (1868), and The Facts of Perception (1878), Introduction to the Lectures on Theoretical Physics (1894).

Hesse, M. 1974: *The Structure of Scientific Inference*. Berkeley, Cal.: University of California Press.

Hull, D. 1974: *Philosophy of Biological Sciences*. Englewood Cliffs, NJ: Prentice-Hall.

Kelly, D. and Kreuger, J. 1984: The psychology of abstraction. *Journal for the theory of Social Behavior*, 14, 43–68.

Kitchner, P. 1984: In defense of intentional psychology. *Journal of Philosophy*, LXXXI (2), 89–106.

Leary, D. 1979: Wundt and after: psychology's shifting relations with the natural sciences, social sciences and philosophy. *Journal of the History of the Behavioral Sciences*, 13, 231-41.

Leary, D. 1980: Immanuel Kant and the development of modern psychology. In Woodward and Ash, 1982, 17–42.

Mach, E. 1883/1959: *Analysis of Sensations*. Chicago Ill.: Dover.

Mandelbaum, M. 1971: *History, Man and Reason*. Baltimore and London: Johns Hopkins University Press.

Manicas, P. T. 1982: The human sciences: a radical separation of psychology and the social sciences. In P. F. Secord, (ed.), *Explaining Human Behavior: consciousness, human action and social structure*. Beverly Hills, Cal. Sage, 155–73.

Manicas, P. T. 1983: Reduction, epigenesis and explanation. *Journal for the Theory of Social Behavior*, 13, 331–52.

Manicas, P. T. and Rosenberg, A. 1985: Naturalism, epistemological individualism and 'The Strong Programme' in the sociology of knowledge. *Journal for the Theory of Social Behavior*, 15, 76–102.

Manicas, P. T. and Secord, P. F., 1983: Implications for psychology of the new philosophy of science. *American Psychologist*, 38, 399–413.

Margolis, J. 1984: *Philosophy of Psychology*. Englewood Cliffs, NJ: Prentice-Hall.

Medawar, P. 1974: A geometric model of reduction and emergence. In Ayala and Dobzhansky, 1974, 57–63.

Mill, J. S. 1930: *Logic*, 8th edition, London: Longmans Green.

Neisser, U. 1976: *Cognition and Reality*. San Francisco: W. H. Freeman.

Passmore, J. 1966: *A Hundred Years of Philosophy*, 2nd revised edition, New York: Basic Books.

Pastore, N. 1974: Reevaluation of Boring on Kantian influence, nineteenth-century nativism, gestalt psychology and Helmholtz. *Journal of the History of Behavioral Sciences*, 10, 365–90.

Pattee, H. H. 1972: Physical problems of decision-making constraints. *International Journal of Neuroscience*, 3, 99–106.

Pattee, H. H. 1973: The physical basis and origin of hierarchical control. In Pattee (ed.), *Hierarchy Theory: the challenge of complex systems*, New York: Braziller.

Pattee, H. H. 1974: The problem of biological hierarchy. In C. H. Waddington, (ed.) *Toward a Theoretical Biology*, Los Angeles, Cal.: University of California Press.

Pattee, H. H. 1976: Physical theories of biological coordination. In Grene and Mendelsohn, 1976, 153–73.

Polanyi, M. 1968: Life's irreducible nature. *Science*, 160, 1308–12. Reprinted in Grene and Mendelsohn, 1976, 128–42.

Pribram, K. H. 1965: Proposals for a structural pragmatism: some neuropsychological considerations of problems in philosphy. In B. Wolman and E. Nagel (eds), *Scientific Psychology: principles and approaches*, New York: Basic Books, 1965.

Pribram, K. H. 1971: *Languages of the Brain*. Englewood Cliffs, NJ.: Prentice-Hall.

Pribram, K. H. 1977: Some comments on the nature of the perceived universe. In Shaw and Bransford, 1977, 83–101.

Pribram, K. H. 1982: Reflections on the place of brain in the ecology of mind. In Weimer and Palermo, vol. 2. 1982.

Pribram, K. H. and Gill, M. M. 1976: *Freud's 'Project' Re-Assessed:* London, Hutchinson.

Rieber, R. W. (ed.) 1980: *Wilhelm Wundt and the making of a Scientific Psychology.* New York: Plenum Press.

Schaffner, K. F. 1976: The Watson-Crick model of reductionism. In Grene and Mendelsohn, 1976, 101–27.

Shaw, R. and Bransford, J. (eds) 1977: *Perceiving, Acting and Knowing: toward an ecological psychology*. Hillsdale, NJ: Lawrence Erlbaum.

Sober, E. 1978: Psychologism. *Journal for the Theory of Social Behavior*, 8, 165–91.

Sperry, R. W. 1976: Mental phenomena as causal determinants in brain functions. In Globus, 1976, 163–78.

Turner R. S. 1977: Herman Helmholtz and the empiricist vision. *Journal of the History of the Behavioral Sciences*, 13, 49–58.

Turner, R. S. 1982: Helmholtz, sensory physiology, and the disciplinary develoment of German psychology. In Woodward and Ash, 1982, 147–66.

Turvey, M. T., Shaw, R. E., Reed, E. S. and Mace, W. M. 1981: Ecological laws of perceiving and acting: in reply to Fodor and Pylyshyn. *Cognition*, 9, 237–304.

Watson, J. B. 1913/1963: Psychology as the behaviorist views it. In W. Dennes (ed.), *Readings in the History of Psychology*. New York: Appleton-Century-Crofts.

Weimer, W. B. 1973: Psycholinguistics and Plato's paradoxes of the Meno, *American Psychologist*, 28, 15–33.

Weimer, W. B. 1975: The psychology of inference and expectation: some preliminary remarks. In G. Maxwell and A. R. Anderson (eds), *Minnesota Studies in the Philosophy of Science*, vol. VI, Minneapolis: University of Minnesota Press, 430–86.

Weimer, W. B. 1976: Manifestations of mind: some conceptual and empirical issues. In Globus et al., 1976, 5–31.

Weimer, W. B. and Palermo, D. S. (eds) 1982: *Cognition and the Symbolic Processes*, 2 vols, Hillsdale, NJ: Lawrence Erbaum.

Weiss, P. A. 1971: *Hierarchical Organized Systems in Theory and Practice*. New York: Hafner.

Wimsatt, W. C. 1976a: Reductionism, levels of organization, and the mind body problem. In Globus et al., 1976, 205–67.

Wimsatt, W. C. 1976b; Complexity and organization. In Grene and Mendelsohn, 1976, 174–93.

Woodward, W. R. 1982: Wundt's program for the new psychology: vicissitudes of experiment, theory, and system. In Woodward and Ash, 1982, 167–97.

Woodward, W. R. and Ash, M. G., (eds) 1982: *The Problematic Science, Psychology in Nineteenth Century Thought*. New York: Praeger.

Wundt, W. 1897 *Outlines of Psychology*, translated with the cooperation of the author by C. H. Judd. Leipzig: W. Engelmann.

4

Social Sources of Mental Content and Order

Rom Harré

Introduction: presumptions of contemporary practice

Much of the practice of contemporary psychology is underpinned by traditional answers to the question 'What is the human mind?' These answers tend to be Cartesian in spirit. 'The mind' is a hidden and closed arena (be it Cartesian substance or Husserlian subjectivity). There occur acts and states, processes and structures, imperfectly manifested in something wholly other, public behavior. While the gross Cartesian thesis that the mind is a substance alien in all its qualities to the substance of the material world is rarely voiced, it is as rarely explicitly repudiated.

Perhaps the choice of question above is in part responsible for the tendency to repeat Cartesian answers. Suppose instead we ask 'What is to have a mind?' This might as easily prompt an answer in terms of capacities and skills as the above question form has prompted an answer in terms of substance. Since we share a great number of material skills with animals the specific character of the human mind, *a fortiori*, cannot be captured by studies that concentrate on material skills alone. I propose to provide an answer to the question posed above in its most specific form, 'What is to have a human mind?' through attention to the most pervasive human practice, conversing. This will not just be a further celebration of the fact that alone among creatures human beings can talk (and some can read and write) but will emerge from reflection on the uses of that capacity and other symbolic possibilities in the public practice of conversation. In short, I hope to recommend the thesis that to have acquired a mind is to have learned to conduct a conversation, and eventually to have picked up the art of conducting some part of the conversation in private.

If public conversation is prior to individual mind, a student of the mind should look for the source of at least some of the properties of mind in features of public conversation. The hypothesis that most of the features of properties of mind are derived from and sometimes actually reducible to features of public conversation, is one of the fundamentals of what I shall call *social constructionism*. However, it is all very well to remark on the parallels and structural similarities between minds and conversation, but how do these analogies and homomorphisms come about? The second fundamental thesis of social constructionism concerns the active role of people makers. The more mature members of human conversational communities teach mindedness to neophytes. Developmental psychology, in my view, is not the mapping of a maturational process merely triggered by occasions of learning, but the charting of a history of indoctrination. The learning of these theories through public conversational practices we apply to ourselves.

All this will come, I hope, to seem entirely obvious as my exposition unfolds. And yet the principles and hypotheses of social constructionism are quite alien to the assumptions underlying much of current psychological practice, both academic and therapeutic. Perhaps Cartesianism is not the only hidden constraint on our attempts to understand human beings. We must also take account of the pervasiveness of individualism. Of course the Cartesian image of a world of atomistic minds, each locked within its own sphere of subjectivity is also an extreme individualism, but something more than reference to a philosophic tenet is needed to explain why psychologists took so long to begin the first tentative flirtations with social constructionism, since the very idea of 'conversation' is a collective concept. Historians have pointed out how much the slide towards experimentation in psychology was exacerbated by the imperatives of the design of testing programs. Testing burgeoned around the time of World War I; recruits, school children and immigrants all were required to display individual intellectual, moral and medically relevant characteristics. Much of the impetus for the development of testing came from the strong eugenics lobby in the USA, but the needs of mass educational systems developing in Europe contributed to the trend. This testing was, so to say, a continuing reproduction of the examination hall. In the interview and examination for an immigrant visa, people are isolated and examined one by one. And this is just what the majority of psychological experiments are like today. 'Cheating is forbidden in the examination hall' is a rule which ensures that the answers in each examination book are the work of that candidate alone. The same rule with the same effect is faithfully reproduced in the instructions to subjects that are part of the methodology of experiments. In so far as therapeutic, occupational and other applied psychologies reinvoke the 'testing' methodology, they too reproduce the traditional school room. Psychology, set within this frame, cannot but take all its concepts – remembering, problem-solving, having attitudes, moral reasoning and so on – individualistically. But that begs the question of whether in the lives people actually lead, remembering, problem-solving, moral reasoning and so on are 'done' by individuals. Social constructionism insists that, in general, they are not. And when they are, the individual process reproduces the structure of the social one. This story is rich in ironies. The late Henri Tajfel mounted a campaign for a European style psychology defined by contrast with the way psychology was practised in the United States. This psychology would place its main emphasis on group interactions. But Tajfel set about trying to base an account of group behavior on individual acts of social comparison, a research program as individualistic as any to be found across the Atlantic. He was in thrall to the experimental methodology, which in reproducing the essential features of the examination hall could not but reproduce the individualism of the assumptions of long-forgotten testing programs. Those who ignore history, as has often been remarked, are fated to repeat it!

Individualism also has a moral aspect. It appears in the practice of assigning moral responsibility for actions to the individuals who are their immediate vehicles, rather than to the firms, families, clubs or other groups to which they belong, and on whose behalf such actions are usually performed. The locus of responsibility for actions varies widely from culture to culture. In the United States individual responsibility is perhaps at a unique peak, while among those Eskimo little affected by contact with Western cultural assumptions it is virtually non-existent. A visitor to the United States, even from so closely allied a culture as the United Kingdom, is immediately struck by the extreme formality of American practices and the rigid insistence on conformity to rule. 'Going by the book' is so pervasive a feature of 'how things are done' that one soon learns to give up the attempt to negotiate a short path through the tangled skein of rules.

Underlying these formal practices is a way of thinking about human beings in their relation to their actions. In willingly accepting the rule of rules a social actor is adopting the form of action of an automaton. When responsibility is handed over to the rule system, an actor is a merely passive vehicle or medium through which the rules are manifested. It is not hard to see that this aspect of individualism (paradoxically appearing as excessive conformity) might lie behind the search for law-like regularities in the laboratory. If the automaton assumption is taken not as social construction but as a metaphysical datum we might have an explanation of much that is puzzling in traditional psychological research. A startling example of what seems to be the influence of an automaton assumption is the way Duval and Wicklund (1972) look for the conditions for helping behavior. They set up an 'experiment' in such a way that all reference to moral issues is deleted. Or, to put the same point another way, the subjects are defined and treated as automata. Of course, in a social order in which there is a high degree of individualism there is a very strong temptation actually to make oneself as automaton-like as possible, and this makes good the metaphysical basis of work such as that of Duval and Wicklund. But the analysis shows that their work is not a successful attempt to discover the lawful regularities of helping behavior. It is actually an explanation of culturally specific ways of managing the excessive demands of a particular moral order; and it itself is a culturally specific way of disclaiming, or at least providing for the disclaiming of, moral responsibility.

The adoption of this social constructionist point of view facilitates the bringing together of cognitive science and psychology with the real work of psychological processes. There may be phenomena, described in psychological terms, that are wholly explicable by reference to social rules, local moral orders and social conventions. Of course, there will be a problem for cognitive science, what do individual people have to be able to do, to know and to follow conventions? But these will probably be quite general skills. All that makes a phenomenon a distinctive psychological phenomenon will be packed into the content of the conventions. I believe 'rationality' to be such an attribute. We will find that understanding rationality requires attention both to individual cognitive processes, of the sort studied by conventional academic psychology, and to social processes involving conventions and rights.

Intimations of the priority of social to individual psychological phenomena

The idea that human psychology is intimately bound up with the social worlds in which human beings develop and live is not new. It was enunciated clearly by George Herbert Mead in his *Mind, Self and*

Society which, though published in 1934, was the record of lectures given in the first part of the century. However, it is only in the last thirty years or so that the idea of language as the mediating phenomenon between society and mind has been clearly identified. For instances, Edward Sapir (1957) says,

> In a sense, the network of cultural patterns of a civilization is indexed in the language that expresses that civilization. (p. 68)

and draws the obvious conclusion that,

> Linguistics may thus hope to become something of a guide to the understanding of the 'psychological geography' of culture in the large. (p. 73)

We are only now beginning to appreciate the anticipation of much of the current development out of Sapir's intuitions that is to be found in the work of Vygotsky, and to a lesser extent in that of Luria (Vygotsky, 1978). However, the full extent of the influence exerted by social matters through the medium of language and other social practices, on the development of the typical minds of the culture, has not been fully exploited.

In this chapter I propose to outline some of the aspects of human psychology which can only be adequately tackled when conceived in the social constructionist way. Part of the constructionist thesis goes beyond the intuition of Sapir and the precocious discoveries of Vygotsky. In his later philosophy, Wittgenstein (1953) made great use of the idea of a 'language game', a practical activity within which the use of language played an essential part. Language games, Wittgenstein supposed, were found in loosely connected clusters he called forms of life.

A form of life involves not only clusters of practices but also moral orders, and I shall have much to say about them in this chapter. By a 'moral order' I mean a system of rights, obligations and duties, by reference to which kinds of actions are distributed among people, considered as belonging to categories – child, politician and so on, and as fulfilling roles – housewife, bank manager and so on.

I propose that we take a journey along the social boundary between individuals, persons, and the collective forms of life. Many aspects of the psychology of individuals are the products of social processes. For example, the repertoire of emotions available to the members of a culture, the subjective organization of thoughts and feeling are, as the unities of self, cultural phenomena mediated by language. There is good reason to think that emotion repertoires, the structures of unity of the self and many other psychological phenomena, differ radically between different human societies. Furthermore, many phenomena which are ascribed to individuals as psychological processes are actually literally social – that is, exist only in patterns of conversational exchange.

In much of the practice of psychology there is an illusion of individuality fostered by unexamined ethnocentric political assumptions and the peculiar experimental methodology that has dominated much of the empirical work in psychology, partly as a consequence of it. For instance, human rationality is actually not an individual phenomenon, a property of mind merely displayed in conversation. It should be understood rather in terms of social conventions for the kinds of speech acts the utterance of which is proper to the holders of certain roles and for the kinds of writing which persons of certain categories are required to adopt for relevant purposes. Similarly, much moral decision making is not a matter of individuals making up their minds about what to do, but is the achievement of public conversations under certain kinds of collective constraints. There are, also, other mental phenomena that take the form of interpersonal social encounters, in which both parts are taken by the same person. For instance, much of what we mean by ascribing agency to individuals is to be understood as the practice of carrying on debates with oneself in the same form as those in which one person seeks, within the conventions of a society, to control another. The way in which we assess the quality of our own beliefs is modelled on the way we judge those of others and others judge our public claims to knowledge. I shall be looking into some of the ways in which, as Goffman put it, the blunt fingers of society enter into and shape the individual mind.

The concept of 'society' and the meaning of qualifying a structure or process as 'social' need elucidating. The most important issue is the matter of scale. Undoubtedly, there are vast macro-processes and consequential structural changes that occur in the ways mankind behaves in the large, of which we have only very shadowy ideas. From the point of view of the social constructionist approach to psychology, we need take account only of local and rather small scale social interactions. The macro-processes and structures of society can most usefully be relegated to a background or selection environment, which might play the same sort of role for social innovations as a relatively stable biological environment does for organic evolution. The kinds of collective activities to which psychologists should direct their attention are personal encounters in more or less bounded episodes occuring within relatively fully-shared social assumptions and moral orders, and of couse mediated by a more or less common language. As I have suggested, it is useful to conceive these encounters in terms of Wittgensteinian language games, social and material practices, such as baptisms, quarrels, trials, house-buildings and so on, in which language and other symbolic systems play an essential role. Conversations in fact are best understood not as linguistic encounters between anonymous culture-free individuals, but organized according to social relations which embody this or that moral order, local systems of rights, obligations and duties.

What is a conversation? Foundations of an alternative ontology

Speech-acts

Conversation analysis has developed as a technical branch of ethnomethodology. But for the purposes of this discussion we do not need so elaborate a treatment.

Think of a conversation as a flow of 'speech-acts'. The idea of a speech-act was first introduced by J. L. Austin (1962). To analyze a conversation in terms of speech-acts is to think of it as consisting of linguistic exchanges between speakers and hearers, effective through the social force of the utterances rather than by virtue of their literal meaning. For example, I recently heard a waitress say 'Do you want to add a tip, Sir?' to a diner who had signed a credit card slip without adding the tip. It was apparent that though literally a query, the answer 'No' was not an option for next utterance. The speech-act had the social force of a reprimand. It is worth noticing that the social force of a speech-act is usually independent of the subjective states of speakers and hearers. One can be held to a promise regardless of one's unexpressed intentions. A speech-act is constituted, we may say, by the intersection of the manifested intentions of the speaker and the manifested uptake of the hearer. The conversation goes on encouraged by smiles, frowns, nods and so on, even when the hearer may be almost unconscious with boredom or thinking of something else. Utterances and expressed understandings create a flow of social acts appropriate to the kind of encounter which the participants believe is taking place. So, for example, in the course of a baptismal ceremony, various speech-acts are uttered and the ceremony moves majestically to its end through the shared acceptance of whatever might be the social force of the utterances of the various persons engaged in the encounter. Most conversations, it should be remembered, are not necessarily perceived to have occurred in the same way or to have achieved the same social ends for all the participants. The conversation is an extremely complex entity which has first its own internal semantic and logical structure, as well as a form which is, so to say, fathered upon it by the various participants. In fact, it would be better to have said that potentially there are as many forms as there are participants. I shall leave aside for the moment that second level of complexity and consider the conversation simply in terms of the shared interpretations of speakers and hearers needed to conduct a conversation at all.

Austin's theory of speech-acts was based upon the idea that conversational utterances could be thought of in terms of three aspects or 'forces'. There was the locutionary aspect, what the utterance meant literally – that is, what it might mean to someone who understood the language but was not privy to the social meanings of the events in question. This includes, of course, the descriptive meaning of the utterance, say 'Shut the door', without which such a command would be impossible of execution. Secondly, there was the illocutionary force, which was the social act performed by the utterance of the words. Finally, there was the perlocutionary aspect, that which the uttering of that speech-act with that illocutionary force brought about as a further effect. For example, the sentence 'Why don't we move into the other room?', is literally a question. But when uttered by a hostess at the close of a dinner party, it has the illocutionary force of an invitation, and if it is successful it will have the perlocutionary force of moving the participants to another part of the house. Perlocutionary forces may be very various. There may be social upshots and even physiological consequences, as for example when a well-directed insult brings a blush to the cheek of the person offended.

The five indexicalities

In Austin's original formulation of the idea of a speech-act, the important qualification which is nowadays called contextuality, that is, the dependence of meaning on the particular occasion of utterance, was largely introduced, indirectly, through examples. The concept of 'indexicality' enables us to give a more refined account of the contextuality of speech-acts.

Indexicality as a property of utterances can be illustrated with a simple example such as 'Put this glass here now'. To understand that utterance fully, the hearer must have some knowledge of and preferably be present at the occasion of its being said. All statements which include indexical expressions like 'this', 'here', 'now', etc. require such participatory knowledge in order to be fully understood. From the point of view of the analysis of conversational utterances of the ordinary, everyday kind, there are five major indexicalities – those of 'where', 'when', 'which', 'who' and 'what'. The indexicals 'here' and 'now', 'there' and 'then', 'this' and 'that' and so on, tie the meaning of utterances to the spatio-temporal locations of their utterance, and so to the persons who utter them. However, for many purposes, particularly with respect to the psychological effects of conversation, the indexicals of physical time and place are of only secondary importance. It is 'who' and 'what' that are dominant. For speakers of English and French, 'who' indexicality is likely to be carried by the pronouns, so that a listener must be present on the occasion of an utterance to know the full meaning of 'I love you' and 'Je t'aime', since in this respect the logical grammar of 'I' is like that of 'this'. 'What' indexicality picks out the original contextual idea, that the illocutionary force of an utterance, what we take it as expressing on a particular occasion, requires knowledge of the social situation, the other speech-acts within the flow of which it has a place as the particular act it is. So, in the examples above, the uttering of a sentence of question form is taken by those present to be an invitation in the context of the dinner. In another context it might be a request for information. So illocutionary force is an indexical feature of speech-acts, just as are spatio-temporal reference and speaker identification.

People-space

This brief analysis will form the basis of a metaphysical myth, a novel ontology intended to elucidate the way in which conversational practices are dominant in many aspects of individual psychology. The physical sciences are based upon a metaphysical scheme in which the beings under study, whatever their specific properties, are laid out in space-time and the interactions by which they constitute a world are thought of as propagated from one space-time location to another. Hypotheses as to the structure of that space-time are an important aspect of physical sciences, as had been made very clear in the recent transition from a flat Euclidean-Newtonian space-time to the anisotropic topologies of relativistic schemes. Can one construct an alternative ontology for the psychological social sciences? From the point of view of the social constructionist, meaning rather than causal interaction is the basic medium of interpersonal relations.

In conversations, basic entities are neither people nor their thoughts, but speech-acts. I hope to show that it is to the conventions governing speech-acts that our investigation of such psychological attributes and processes in rationality, decision making and so on, can usefully be redirected. Features of our psychologies, concealed by the metaphysics of things in space-time, are revealed by the shift to an ontology of speech-acts. It might, then, be a useful fiction to base research programs on the assumption of a universe of speech-acts located in a people space. A people-space, as a manifold of discrete points, makes speakers into places – locations for speech-acts. The array of people is to be thought of as the space in which the forces of speech-acts as entities interact and move. The development of this myth will help to bring out certain features of human interaction which are obscured by the scientistic location of human pychology in the metaphysical scheme of the physical sciences – obscured, that is, by the assumption that psychology must be the study of processes in complex things located in Newtonian space-time. Does people-space have a structure? Or is it merely flat, isotropic, the same in all directions? One obvious aspect in which people-space is anisotropic is due to there being an unequal distribution of the rights, obligations and duties to utter certain kinds of speech-acts relative to the social roles and categories a person may from time to time occupy. For example, a Catholic has a duty to confess, the priest has a reciprocal duty to listen, to order penance and to give absolution. If one thinks of the confessional in speech-act terms it is obvious that the speech-acts of different categories flow differentially through the people-space, depending upon the role-status of given speakers and listeners. People who do not have the right to speak but are still noticeably present as persons may be thought of as empty places in people-space, and so on (see Harré, 1983). This brings us to the idea of a moral order.

What is a moral order? I shall be using the term to refer to a system of role-related rights, obligations and duties. Amongst the elements of a moral order are the conventions manifested in certain conversational practices, like silences, like the structures of conversation to be seen in interrogation, confessionals, and the like. Associated with this, and intimately involved in the way in which roles are related to rights, is a system of criteria for evaluating the quality of actions and the worth of people. These criteria, or rather judgments in accordance with them, are marked or manifested in rituals expressing the respect or contempt of people for one another. For the purposes of this discussion, such rituals may be confined to small-scale encounters. As suggested, the effect of moral orders is to structure people-space with respect to the kinds of speech-acts that can flow through that system. One can go further. A system of beliefs and conventions must lie behind the practices described. We may well ask where those beliefs and conventions are to be located. It would be far too naive a psychologism to suppose (without further ado) that they are no more than the shared competences of individual human beings. A good case may be made for saying that some beliefs and conventions are actually located in the practices themselves and, ontologically speaking, exist only in the conversation. But that possibility would take us too far afield for our present purpose.

Conversational entities

If my myth of an alternative ontology is to be taken seriously, a subtle issue, of some philosophical technicality, must be tackled. A reader whose inclination verges to the psychological need not pause at this point, but pass directly on to the next section.

Having refined our notion of people-space in terms of a structure imposed by moral orders, we need to clarify the other main element of the metaphysical scheme, namely, the entities analogous to the thing-individuals of the Newtonian ontology. The suggestion for this development I owe to Jonathan Bennett, who pointed to the unsatisfactory vagueness of talk of speech-acts as persisting entities moving through people-space.

The question then is 'What is the nature of that which moves from person to person, say in the spread of gossip?' As some canard spreads around a small town each townsperson whispers something like 'Did you know that George has lost all his money?' in that specially hushed tone that is reserved for the speech-act of character assassination. As Bennett pointed out, for n townspeople there are n utterances of tokens of the sentence type 'Did you know that G?' Each utterance is at its own place in people-space and never at any other. Nothing has moved. At best one might have a kind of cinematographic illusion of motion. Here, we might forge an ontology on the basis of the distinction between action and act. Each of these similar utterances is a unique action and they are many. But each is the substratum of an act which, remaining self-identical, moves. In speech-act terminology, each utterance has the same *force*, the belittling of Mr N. N. So while the utterances of the sentence-tokens are numerically distinct and stationary, more or less qualitatively identical, the force or social act accomplished by each token utterance is numerically identical as it passes along the array of discrete points of the people-space. It is *one* belittling.

This metaphysical problem has analogues in other fields. What is 'the gene' which is numerically identical as *it* is passed from generation to generation? Each organism in a family of descent has a numerically distinct molecular realization of 'it', as the gene which passes on cannot be a material molecular arrangement. But in each generation that token of the type of molecular arrangement has the same, numerically the same, genetic power, in that 'it' produces the same (qualitatively identical but numerically distinct) phenotypic structure in the members of each generation. Genetic information is another name for genetic power. The molecular gene is the non-heritable (that is, stationary) material substrate for the numerically identical information which moves, unchanged, through the generations. In physics we are inclined to say that it is the same (numerically the same) energy which was in the glass of hot water and now is in the air. The motions of the several collections of molecules are the numerically distinct material substrates for that sameness.

'A' cheer issuing from the throats of a hundred thousand enthusiastic supporters is a speeech-act of confirmation for the views of the demagogue who is addressing them. Is it one speech-act of confirmation covering a large area of people-space, or is it many such acts? I propose to maintain consistency with the above proposal to solve the problem of motion, by opting for the former. Just as one thing can extend over many points of Newtonian space, so one speech-act can extend over many points in people-space. This illustrates the ontological distinction between utterings (actions) and acts (the social force of those utterings). The universe of conversation is built of acts.

Are the aforesaid forces particulars? They are clearly not material particulars, as utterances would be if set back in the Newtonian metaphysical scheme. But in the conversational ontology the issue of whether a being is a particular – reference to some material criterion – is an irrelevant one. It is clear that *an* insult, indexically tied to you and me and individuated by that indexicality and content, is an instance (token) of a type, that of jocular insults. But in the Newtonian ontology, the basic particulars are utterances, and in that ontology speech-acts are types.

This discussion can also be seen as a way of introducing two basic metrical concepts for people-space, distance and spread. 'Distance' is the number of people-places through which a speech-act must pass to reach its locus of intent and provoke effective action – as an order passes from commander, through junior officers, to the man in the field. But the order reaches more points in people-space as it moves. The measure of this is 'spread'.

A Cartesian residue

The Cartesianism of the received tradition is an implicit ontology, to which the 'metaphysics of conversation' stands as an alternative. The trouble with the Cartesian scheme is that it seems to lead to the inescapable conclusion that the minds of others are inaccessible. Yet the project of psychology seems to be to achieve a scientific understanding of the properties of this myriad of inaccessible entities, human minds. Set in the alternative framework of the conversational ontology, much of the apparent inaccessibility dissolves. The close tie between the uses of language, moral orders and psychological phenomena resolves the self-stultifying aspects of Cartesianism as a metaphysics for psychology. Reasoning, emotions, memory and so on can be studied without the threat of the scepticism that infects any hypothetico–deductive theorizing, for it is only within the practice of scientific theorizing that any scientific accounts of the inaccessible are possible.

As pointed out by Georges Ray, in discussion, however, there is one class of psychological phenomena which resist this treatment and remain obdurately subjective, in the sense of accessible only in one consciousness. These are the qualities of our experience, the feeling of pain, the hue of a red apple, the timbre of a clarinet in the chalumeau register. But do these 'qualities' constitute a problem field for any future psychology? An argument of Wittgenstein's can be adapted to support the setting aside of this aspect of human experience as in principle resistant to scientific inquiry. Wittgenstein pointed out that the public use of sensation words, color words, sound words, and so on would not be possible if their meaning was created by ostensive definition, only in the presence of the subjective feeling. Each of us would have an unstable and idiosyncratic vocabulary which would never be systematically matched with that of another speaker to enable a conversational exchange. Pain talk becomes meaningful only in the public context of expressing discomfort, in discussions of the exact location of the feeling, in metaphorical description which draws on typical causes of pain and so on. Without public expressions of pains and other feelings, there would be no vocabulary in which to set up a psychological research program into the subjective aspects of individual experience. There is a Cartesian side to each of the minds of mankind. But the very conditions of its inaccessibility precludes the possibility of its investigation.

Nevertheless, there is one branch of psychology where useful but indirect research into qualia is possible: physiological psychology. The pains whose existence is tied to speech-acts and other intensional behavior in public conversation are often, but not always, clearly relatable to distinctive disturbances in the nervous system – 'firing of the c-fibres' as Searle (1984) likes to say. A physiological psychologist could pursue the question of whether anesthesia actually inhibits pain or merely erases the memory of it, by 'on line' studies of the patterns of neural excitation of anesthetized patients. No definitive answer to the question 'Are anesthetized patients really in pain?' could be forthcoming, however, but at least a plausible hypothesis, doomed to remain forever hypothetical in some measure, is capable of being empirically supported. And the neurological analogy argument seems to me to be quite legitimate in discussions of the existence and quality of subjective states of animals. The existence of chronic pain, fibromyalgia and similar complaints, invoking pain without discernible lesions, currently forbids too promiscuous a use of physiological inductions. But they too may be susceptible of a similar treatment, linking instances of types of physiological phenomena, tied to pain, by investigations of standard cases.

To illustrate the social constructionist thesis, I propose to work through two examples in some detail – the emotions and the self. These are chosen because they clearly involve both individuals and the social order – or at least I hope to demonstrate that.

Syntax and the structure of experience: grammar and the self

Persons and selves

Hume's discovery of the systematic elusiveness of the self, that 'unity' of which all a person's thoughts, feelings, memories, decisions, actions and so on are predicated, led him to a 'mere bundle' theory of the mind. Minds are just sequences of atomistic experiences unified only by likenesses and differences between successive but disjoint ideas and impressions. The unity of a mind does not consist in some persistent inner being of which the contents of a mind are all properties. Philosophical psychology has tried to live with the problematic consequences of this proposal ever since. It is in part the apparent inescapability but obvious absurdity of the 'mere bundle' theory that has spawned the many attempts by philosophers to discover the principle of personal identity.

The unities of mind which appear as the sense of temporal continuity, of a common and continuous point of view and of action, are to be understood as the result of syntheses of unmarked fragments of thought, feelings and percepts. In the very process of being grasped as such they are ordered into a unified mind. What sort of unity is this? It is more like the unity of a story than like the unity of a thing. Thoughts are not parts of the mind, but moments in a narrative, the author of which is myself. The episodes of the story each person tells of – and to – himself or herself are unified by virtue of the fact that each person deploys a concept of self and indulges in the socially inculcated practice of self-predication. There is no 'self' if it is conceived as an elusive being that Hume searched for but could not find.

This idea leaves two connected but unsolved problems. From whence is the unifying concept of self derived? And what accounts for the form of the practices of self-predication? Kant thought it was the active but noumenal self that synthesized the unordered manifold of experience into the structure he called the 'transcendental unity of apperception'. This he supposed is the structure which enables a person to contemplate the facts of his own mental life as his. I believe, on the contrary, that it is the people makers of a culture who are responsible for the synthesis of self. By teaching a suitable grammar and by inculcating the practices of self-assessment favored in that culture, they make possible the kind of unity found in the minds of their culture. In the Judaeo-Christian tradition, a person is as much morally responsible for his or her private thoughts and feelings as for those that are publicly manifested in overt actions and sayings. One would expect there to be a common form to the private and public discourses of members of this tradition – in which one's own thoughts and intentions as well as the sayings and actions of others are assessed.

A culture in which personal thoughts and feelings counted for little against the importance of public and collective behavior would hardly be expected to have developed the grammatical means to facilitate reflexive thought. The concept of 'person', publicly identifiable and individuatable, morally responsible only as a member of a collective, would do nicely for such a culture. No grammar more elaborate than that would be needed to facilitate the indexical marking of speeches as those of this or that public person.

But in private and personal contemplation, as a member of my own culture, which has carried much of its traditional moral practices into a secular civilization, I consider myself to function within the same conceptual framework as others take me to occupy and which I take them to occupy. The *concept* of 'self' as the bearer of 'inner unity' should therefore be studied as an analogue of the social concept of 'person', since persons are the public loci of clusters of publicly accountable actions and speeches. One might express this proposal in the metaphor of 'theorizing'. One might say that the personal Kantian syntheses come about through the learning of a theory, a theory that I am a self. I learn this theory by picking up a concept modeled on that of the public person, as that concept is understood in my culture. And of course, I pick up the concept of self in the course of acquiring the linguistic and moral practices of my community. This is a proposal only, a hypothesis to account for the persistent but culturally necessary illusion of selfhood. In order to support it, however, I turn now to highlight some features of the logical grammar of self-appraisal – one practice among those during the learning of which the 'inner self' theory of personal unity may be acquired.

The public concept of 'person' can be used without presuming that the beings taken as persons have complex mental lives. Its use certainly does not presuppose that a person must be able to know that their current experiences are theirs. A remark like 'I'm tired' could have much of its usual force in a public conversation even if the speaker lacked the linguistic resources and self-reflexive capacity to formulate the thought that I know that I am tired. The utterance 'I know that I'm tired' might be used to refute the suggestion that one was staggering about because one was drunk. I follow Strawson (1959) in the idea that we can pick out persons through their possession of capacities for the ascription of experiences, thoughts, intentions and so on in public discourse both to the speaker and others. I do not want to go beyond the public and collective contexts of avowals and expressive remarks. Speech-acts in the first person, involving psychological predicates, are part of the expression of feelings, opinions, intentions and so on. For Strawson, the concept of 'person' is primitive. It is used in such a way that a person can attribute psychological predicates to himself or herself in exactly the same sense as he or she can attribute them to others. This principle does not express a discovery in empirical semantics. It expresses a necessary condition for psychological predicates to have a meaning in a public language. The same concept of 'tiredness' informs 'I am tired', 'You are tired', and 'He is tired'. The differences between these statements are manifold but equivocation of meaning is not among them. The fact that they can be used to perform rather different speech-acts demonstrates only a difference of social roles; there may be no difference among them in descriptive content, but the grounds on which I make a public declaration of *my* condition (tiredness), my moral feelings (anger), my intentions and so on, are systematically different from those upon which I describe, accuse or commiserate with, you. In order to maintain the identity of meaning of a basically constant psychological predicate in all these diverse contexts of use (and so insure public intelligibility of psychological discourses), it is necessary to develop a semantic theory that does not reduce the meaning of psychological predicates to the evidence or grounds upon which they are rightly ascribed. I shall not even begin to undertake such a project here.

Does it follow that the referents of the 'person'-marking expressions in a conversation are just publicly identified embodied human beings? As I have suggested, our cultural and linguistic practices involve a secondary formation in the organization of belief and experience. The pronouns we use for persons have dual uses. Amongst our linguistic resources are the means for formulating queries of the form 'Does he know he is digging the garden?' which might be used should we suspect he is sleep-walking. Or we might want to express doubts about his moral sensibility with 'Does he care he is standing on my foot?' In the latter case there may be no doubt that he is aware of the location of his foot, but is he aware of the moral turpitude of his unremedied posture? Equally, there are many occasions on which remarks like 'I must really do something about my diet!' or 'I must try to be less irritable with him' have a place in our private discourse.

Consider again the simple remark 'I'm tired'. It may be uttered as a complaint. As such it is just a move in a public game. No particular organization of the speaker's experience and systems of belief or memory, etc. is required by the speaker's capacity to make good use of the sentence. The speaker might treat his actions as obedience to the demands of the Gods, as Jaynes suggests once occurred. He may, on the contrary, think of himself as an independent agent, with an intense reflexive awareness of his own states of mind. In the latter case the utterance could be read as a report of an experience. Not only is it an excuse, it is also a description of a condition the speaker realizes is amongst *his* thoughts and feelings. Tiredness is to be fitted in amongst lots of other feelings, memories, thoughts and so on.

Wittgenstein's distinction between first-person uses of psychological predicates, usually marked as the contrast between avowals and descriptions, is required by the need to explain how psychological predicates can have a common meaning in a public language. No one could learn how to use the word 'joy' if what it meant was some subjective feeling and only that. It must like any other word be learnt in a public context. My use of the word 'joy' cannot, then, be just a report of the way I feel, based on the evidence of some subjective state. According to Wittgenstein, it must be learnt as part of the expression of joyfulness.

In saying 'How joyful I feel today!', I am not just describing my inner state, I am expressing my emotion. Of course, amongst my reasons for saying such a thing may be how I feel, but that cannot be its meaning. By contrast, my saying 'He's joyful' is a judgment about his condition (though not necessarily just about his subjective state), based on how he behaves and the sort of remarks he makes in this context. While my expression of my joy may be sincere or insincere, my description of his condition will be true or false. This is a general feature of human conversation.

The way private experience is organized, and particularly the way it is unified by the theory of selfhood entertained by the being in question, will determine how that experience can be located within the mind of an individual person. There may be great cultural differences in the way certain experiences – say, the realization that one has the solution to a problem – are fitted into the ordered flow of thought. Those Greeks who believed in inspiration from the Muses would have taken no personal responsibility for a certain kind of thought, nor credit either.

If actions are ascribed to persons, the evaluations of actions can be transferred to persons if we introduce the concept of moral responsibility. To put the matter in psychological terms, the community must subscribe to the theory that persons are those beings who act intentionally. Much philosophical work remains to be done to link the idea of acting with the possibility of finding grounds for ascriptions of responsibility. We would need to be able to substantiate the claim, in psychological terms, that on a particular occasion a person could have done other than he did. The link is conceptuual rather than empirical, but to establish this intuition an analysis of the concept of agency is needed. (See Harré, 1983.) Moral responsibility arises in a society by way of people coming to believe that they are agents.

Self-assessment must surely be facilitated by the existence of certain grammatical possibilities, possibilities that allow for the framing of a discourse in which one's own avowals can be treated like the descriptions one gives of others.

Epistemic qualifications of perceptual claims

On the avowal theory, 'I can see a fish in the pool' is not a description of a mental state, but an indexically marked annoncement of how the world looks from my point of view. The use of 'I' is wholly explicable in terms of its indexical role in tying the speech-act to the speaker.

What happens when doubts assail me? The honest and sincere speaker epistemically qualifies his or her statement with one of a wide range of propositional attitude expressions. Thus, 'I think I can see a fish in the pool' is a qualified assertion that there is a fish in the pool. The use of the initial 'I' is explicable in terms of its indexical function, the same indexical function as the initial 'I' of the unqualified statement. Philosphers are familiar with the idea that in the context of this kind of utterance, the embedded sentence has a different logical grammar from that of its unqualified use. The referential force of 'fish' is suspended since the truth or falsity of statements made with the complex sentence does not depend on the truth or falsity of the embedded statement. What about the embedded pronoun? Is its indexical force suspended? I claim that it behaves like 'He' in 'He can see a fish in the pool'. It is the shift into the descriptive mode that makes room for the expressed doubt to creep in. If I begin to assess my perceptual claims rather than just expressing them, then I have begun to treat myself as an 'other'. It is this shift that is marked by the adoption of the complex form. The whole complex sentence can be used to make qualified avowals, but the epistemic warrant for the use of the embedded sentence can be scrutinized by the very speaker. But to what does the embedded 'I' refer? An elegant account of this kind of discourse would require the coindexicality of both the uses of 'I'. But the epistemic qualifications expressed seem to need a consideration of the propriety and correctness or otherwise of ascribing a certain state of knowledge, or even some subjective property, to the referent of the embedded pronoun. It is this difference in function which opens up space enough for the theory of 'inner selves' to get a grip. A rival account would have it that the complex qualified avowal is an expression of the speaker's assessment of a subjective condition, a state of the self. From a philosophical point of view, surely the coindexicality account is to be preferred. It shows that these 'inner selves' need not be invoked to explain the possibility of practices of self-assessment. But neither can the coindexical account alone exclude the less parsimonious metaphysics. From a psychological point of view, one must acknowledge the persistence of the inner-self theory as a rival basis for practices of self-assessment. It is that very theory that we imbibe with the grammar of our language and our custom of trying to lay the blame for social disturbances on individuals.

Complex weak performatives

There are several kinds of complex performatives that can be used to illustrate this point. We use expressions like 'Yes, I follow you', both to express encouragement – that is, with perlocutionary force – and sometimes to describe our state of mind. If the expression is given a performative reading the speaker continues happily with his or her exposition. But if it is given a descriptive reading the main speaker is within his rights to ask (aggressively) for proof. What happens when the simple utterance is qualified with 'I think . . .' or some other expression of reserve? Consider the avowal 'I'm going to throw up!' (A). It, too, has a descriptive use, avowing a certain somatic state. But it is also used as a warning, and most people who hear such a remark would so take it. Compare it with 'I think I'm going to throw up!' (B). B is clearly a weaker warning than A. If B is challenged with 'Are you sure?' the grounds offered for the sincerity for B would also be the (less than conclusive) evidence for A. When the sentence-form 'I'm going to throw up!' is embedded in B, it is no longer a performative but a descriptive statement, subject to the same considerations as 'he is going to throw up!', that is, it can be discussed epistemically with respect to the reasons for believing it true. Its performative force is suspended.

This set of relationships is a very common feature of much of our talk. 'I think I'm falling in love with you' is primarily a weaker declaration than 'I'm falling in love with you', and as such has to be considered for its felicity conditions like any other utterance. But these felicity conditions include the epistemic conditions for the embedded sentence now functioning primarily in the descriptive mode. Of what are these descriptions predicated? I believe, in our culture, we absorb a theory of selfhood which encourages us to think that they are ascriptions of mental properties to an inner self. The argument of this section, then, is intended to show that while the 'self' has the grammatical status of a thing, its ontological status may be left quite open: it is no different from the putative referents of the many theoretical terms around which the deepest branches of physical science are built.

The problem I have been addressing in this section could be put like this: the traits, beliefs, recollections, feelings and so on of each person may be thought of as a kind of list. What makes it *one* list? I have been suggesting that we both express and create the unity by deploying a concept of self. But there is no self, only the organizational unity of the list. Furthermore, the concept of self that facilitates the organization of the list is itself no more than another item on that list. Nevertheless, the concept of self is related to a real being, the public person. It is on the concept of that being that the concept of self is modelled.

Theoretical concepts used in the natural sciences are usually created by a chain of similes and metaphors. They are supported by analogies, systems of predicates, judgments of likenesses and differences. 'Natural selection' is a concept devised by analogy from that of 'domestic selection' by the judicious deletion of some similarities and emphasis on others. Even in the most esoteric domain of high-energy physics, such as quantum field theory, the juggling of analogies is the main semantic process by which theoretical concepts like 'intermediate vector boson' are created. Failure to grasp the structure of the cluster of similarities and differences upon which the intelligibility of theoretical concepts is based, can lead to disastrous (and occasionally creative) misunderstandings. It is within this kind of account of the semantics of theoretical concepts that we must locate the study of the concept of self – in particularly the study of its relation to the concept of the public person.

Vocabulary and the making of experience: emotions and emotion words

Some uses of emotion words

It will emerge from the discussion that follows that it is a mistake to suppose that there are native (or 'natural') emotions, found amongst all human beings. Nativism is just another example of the ethnocentrism of much current psychological research. There are various *metaphorical uses* of our vocabulary of emotion words for roughly corresponding social and psychological phenomena of other cultures and distant epochs. The first step to a more sophisticated theory will be to show how, in research, priority must be given to obtaining a proper understanding of how various emotion vocabularies are used. Recent work (Warner, 1986) has shown that the very idea of an emotion as a response suffered by a passive participant in some emotive event is itself part of the social strategies by which emotions and emotion declarations are used by people in certain interactions. This is not to deny that there are 'leakages' into consciousness from raised heart beat, increased sweating, swollen tear ducts and so on. But these effects are incidental to what it is to be in this or that emotional state. It turns out that the dominant contribution comes from the local social world, by way of its linguistic practices and the moral judgments in the course of which emotions are defined. Ironically, the naive ideas of such as Plutchik (1980), that there is a small number of universal or basic emotions, is demonstrably a consequence of an unthinking individualism. Adopting a more realistic point of view opens up the possibility that, quite often, emotions can exist only in the reciprocal exchanges of a social encounter. The new approach to the study of an emotion, say benevolence or anger, suggests that instead of asking 'What is anger?' (a question which regards the recognition of anger as unproblematic and so incorporates unexamined commonsense), we should first ask 'How is the *word* "anger" used in *this* kind of encounter among people of *this* kind?

Looking first at the uses of words not only sensitizes the investigator to his or her own ethnocentric presuppositions, it also allows for the possibility that other cultures may use closely related concepts in very different ways. There may be cultures in which, though the term in question comes, so to speak, under the same umbrella, it is involved in the creation of quite different expectations and incorporates quite different moral judgments. But reliance on unexamined commonsense understanding has another unfortunate effect that the linguistic turn can help prevent. There has been a tendency to embed as paradigm cases studies of a small repertoire of rather simple emotions within the entire practice of psychology. Not surprisingly, given the conceptuual naivety of much psychological research, these paradigmatic emotions turn out to be those that have an easily identified and easily measured physiological aspect. For example, in one well-known text book, only depression, anxiety, lust and anger are mentioned! Lust and depression are not emotions. Depression is a mood, and lust a bodily agitation. We are left with anxiety and anger. 'Anxiety' may sometimes be used to refer to an emotion but it is a generic term, with a wide and vaguely bounded usage. Despite the brilliant studies by Aristotle in *Rhetoric* and Averill (1982), anger is often studied as if it were nothing but a state of the physiological system, coupled with an overt ethological display.

To illustrate the power of an earlier linguistic study I borrow, in simplified form, Sabini and Silver's classic account (1982) of envy and jealousy, the main 'green' emotions. Under what conditions do we use the *words* 'envy' and 'jealousy'? In asking this we mean to consider the rules and conventions for carrying on those complex practices Wittgenstein called 'language games'. Here is one possibility – a language game in which 'envy' and 'jealously' have distinctive conditions of application. (Sometimes they seem to be used almost synonymously.) The following conditions have to obtain if B is to be properly said to be envious of A. A has possession of some good X and, generally speaking, all else being equal, B concedes that A has a right to X. B himself would like to have X, though not necessarily to deprive A of it. There are two kinds of envy, benign and sinful or malicious. The reason B is envious of A (in the malicious sense) is that he takes A's possession of X to be demeaning to himself, B. B may apply various remedies. He may claim that A is not really worthy of X, so after all A's having it does not so much demean B but shows up as corrupt of foolish those who have awarded X to A. Alternatively B might set about minimizing the value of X. A's having it isn't really demeaning to B because after all X is really worthless. We would be inclined to say that B was jealous of A when each had some prior right to X. B may think that only he has a proper right to X and that A has deprived him of his rightful possession or the like. If he is jealous, B will adopt characteristically different strategies from those relevant for malign envy. B might go so far as to destroy X or even to kill A, failing to regain X legitimately. B's envy may be benign, as when he is delighted that A has received X, thinks that A deserves it, and perhaps a little wistfully hopes one day to have an X himself.

What does this brief analysis of the differential uses of a vocabulary show? It makes abundantly clear that the study of envy and jealousy will require careful attention to the details of local systems of rights and obligations, of criteria of value and so on. In short, these emotions cannot be seriously studied without attention to the local moral order. That moral order is essential to the existence of just those concepts in the cognitive repertoire of the community. The point can be illustrated by reference to some recent work of Nadia Reissland. She found that the mothers of small children were unable to say whether quarrelling children were envious or jealous of each other. At first she thought this showed that the concepts were not clearly distinguished in the linguistic community of the mothers. We devised a little test to see. They were asked to imagine three characters N, M and O. N and M are seated at an outdoor cafe, very jolly together, sipping Pernod, say. O sees them from across the street. In the first scenario, M is married to N, while in the second M is married to O. Unhesitatingly, the group thought that O would be envious of N in the first case, but jealous in the second. Here is a very simple example of the role of a moral order in the differential use of a pair of emotion words. How do we explain the mothers' original difficulty? The mothers had no idea what moral order obtained with regard to matters in dispute amongst their children, the communal toys of a university developmental psychology department.

There are many other language games in which the words 'envy', 'envious', 'jealous' and so on play a part. For example, 'envious' can be used to express congratulations and avow a wish, as in 'I am envious of your trip to Athens'. Then there is the dog-in-the-manger use of 'jealous'. 'Guard this jealously', that is 'Don't let anyone else get at it.' This is close to the pathological sense of jealousy we ascribe to a woman who makes a scene if her husband 'so much as looks at another woman' (and of course vice versa).

One must commend the work of Averill (1982), who anticipated much of what we are here advocating. Averill begins with Aristotle's idea that anger is an agitation brought on by some form of moral transgression, and then goes on to develop that notion in contemporary contexts. He builds up a theory of the use of the concept on the basis of an analysis of the local moral order and depends on his implicit knowlege of the language game of anger attributions. Anger, like envy and jealousy, is a generic emotion – or perhaps it would be best to say a cluster of emotions – with diverging species in a number of distinctive language games. Here are brief sketches of three.

There is the case where somebody's actions are interpreted as gross violations of the injured party's moral status (for instance, an affront to dignity). Depending on the level of moral transgression the emotion may range from annoyance to righteous indignation. In its pathological forms, this genus of emotion includes the taking of umbrage and being in a huff.

Then there is the more complex case of 'nourishing' anger (see Warner, 1986). In this language game the anger 'felt' by the apparently injured party (A) is the (almost) exclusive basis for A's interpretation of the actions of B as transgressions against A's rights, dignity or the like. If A feels annoyed then this is the best ground for holding that B's actions must have been offensive. Furthermore, if B tries to escape from the 'no win' situation by denying any ill intention, then A has further cause of complaint and ground for indignation. B's defense implies that B (offensively) believes that A is the kind of person who would impose unjust interpretations on B's actions or facial expressions, just to nourish his or her anger (see Harré, 1979, for further analyisis of such 'traps').

Finally, there is a relatively new 'anger' language game that is played in T-groups and Rogerian therapy sessions. 'Let's let all that *anger* out!' This kind of talk suggests that there is a buried affective state, a kind of emotional boil, that can be lanced and the poison removed. But even a brief encounter with 'encounter' groups shows that there is almost certainly no such thing as 'buried anger'. The anger displayed by the members seems to be created by the therapy session itself. So the use of word 'anger' in this and related language games bears only a weak family resemblance to its use in the more traditional cases cited above.

These language games involve a whole lexicon or cluster of related verbal expressions such as 'fed up with', 'mad at', 'furious with', together with an elaborate repertoire of para-linguistic displays built up as a culturally distinctive refinement and extension of the native possibilities of ethological display.

The extent to which local moral orders are involved in human emotions suggests that there might be considerable cultural variety in the emotion repertoires of different peoples and epochs. A very simple case can be found in the writings of Prince Peter of Greece, concerning the polyandrous societies of the eastern Himalayas. He noticed that the concepts corresponding to 'envy' and 'jealousy' were not used in the management of sexual relations, but they had an important role in the language games involved in property disputes.

Conditions of word-use as a theory of the emotions

Summarizing much recent work (see also Leventhal, 1980), we can set up a three-component theory of the conditions for the use of emotion words:

1   Many emotion words are called for only if there is some bodily agitation. These words cannot be names for the agitation since it has been clearly demonstrated that qualitatively one and the same agitation can be involved in many different emotions. The James-Lange theory could perhaps be explained as the result of concentrating on this component alone. Many emotions are manifested in typical behavior displays. Such displays are strongly influenced by cultural conventions. However, it would be a mistake to include them amongst the conditions for the use of emotion words. They are, together with the utterance of emotion words, amongst the very forms of expressive display, and as such must share the deep grammar of emotion words themselves.

2   All emotions are intentional – that is, they are 'about' something, in a very general sense. We are afraid of . . . , mad at . . . , jealous of . . . , chagrined because . . . , sad about . . . , grieved for . . . , proud of . . . and so on. In some cases some cognitive work has to be done to seek out the cause of a bodily perturbation. This is particularly true of those emotions that involve the flooding of the system with adrenalin. It would, however, be a mistake to see the work of Schachter (1971) concerning this matter as a proof of a cognitive theory of the emotions. His work on the role of presumed causes in the identification of emotion is really a special case of the general logical point that emotion words (states) are intentional. Some belief in the existence of a suitable intentional object is a necessary

condition for its correct use. Sometimes the identification of the intentional object of an emotion state does involve cognitive 'work', but not always.

3 Finally, the involvement of the local moral order both in the differentiation of emotions and in the situationally relative pre- and proscription of emotions indicates that there is a third set of conditions for the use of emotion words – namely, local systems of rights, obligations, duties and conventions of evaluation.

Must all three conditions be met for the use of all emotion words? There are many cases where all three seem to be involved. For instance, 'anger' seems to be correctly used in some central cases only when there is a distinctive felt bodily agitation, when there is some action by another at which we can be angry, and when that action is able to be construed as a transgression. The qualification 'able to be construed' inserted into the third clause is needed to widen the theory to include the common phenomenon of 'nourishing' anger, described in detail above. But there are also some emotion words whose conditions of use seem to collapse to just the moral criterion. Linda Wood (1983) has shown that there is no specific feeling, nor is it likely that there is a specific cortical state, associated with the emotion of loneliness. Nor is there any standard behavioral display of loneliness. Wood found that those who complained of feeling lonely said in effect that they were more isolated than people of their sort (for instance, grandmothers) ought to be. Actual isolation, measured in terms of human encounters per day, was not so important in complaints of loneliness. The local moral order is the dominant factor here.

Pride is another puzzling emotion, at least if one tries to understand it within the old paradigm. There does not seem to be a distinctive bodily feeling. Instead, the somatic component seems to be derived from culturally idiosyncratic displays of this emotion. There is certainly an intentional object of one's pride and only on condition that one has been worthy of 'victory' is it right to display a proper pride. Overstepping that mark can lead to accusations of hubris or vainglory. But we do say that someone is puffed up or swollen with pride, too. These metaphors may perhaps be traced to an element of the ridiculous in an exaggerated or excessive display. The matter deserves more research. The same could be said for 'hope', which also benefits from a cluster of characteristic metaphors, such as 'surging', 'springing' and the like. There are yet other non-standard cases. Chagrin is the sort of feeling we get when we have publicly set ourselves to achieve something and then have been forced to admit we cannot carry it through. There has been a 'dent to our pride'. Is there a special bodily sensation? I doubt it, despite the usual practice of speaking of chagrin as a feeling. Nor do I think there is a characteristic display. There is often something 'hang-dog' about someone who makes a public ass of himself. But many other pictures could be adopted, partly depending on the extent to which one has 'laid it on the line' in undertaking a given task in the first place. The more over-confident the attempt, the more humiliating the failure. A modest demeanor is a good preparation for winning or losing in our culture.

I have been trying to build up a case, not only in support of a more complex psychological theory of the emotions than the intellectually anorexic accounts offered by academic psychology, but also in support of the claim that two social matters impinge heavily on the personal experience of emotion. These are the local language and the local moral order. The philosophical analysis of the emotion concepts carried by local vocabularies is supposed to reveal the deep grammatical rules by which we can express the conventions for their use. If this is to serve as a basis for a reformed and enlarged psychology it seems to open up the possibility that there are culturally diverse emotion systems and repertories. Historians and anthropologists have established conclusively that there are historically and culturally diverse emotion vocabularies. I claim that it follows that there are culturally diverse emotions.

The cultural relativity of emotions

There are several modes of cultural variation among emotion systems.

1   The inversion of a standard of valuation: In one of the ways we use 'fear' it is used to express an emotion proper to a context of threat or danger, when the intentional object of the fear is generally unambiguous. Fear belongs in a cluster of concepts along with 'bravery' and 'cowardice', which refer to typical culturally relative moral qualities. It may seem hardly worth remarking that in our culture the former is highly approved and the latter condemned. But as Catherine Lutz (1985) has shown, among the Ifaluk the word 'metagu' is used in contexts that share some features with those in which we use terms from the 'fear' vocabulary, in particular the presence, real or imagined, of a threatening or dangerous object. But in other ways the concept of 'metagu' is very different from 'fear'. Among the Ifaluk, those who flee are commended while those who stand their ground are condemned.

The moral qualities with which the concepts are associated are such that it would surely be a gross mistranslation to treat '*metagu*' as equivalent to 'fear'.

2   The encouragement by one culture of what is suppressed by another: The Japanese are said to value and to encourage a peculiar form of 'sweet dependence'. This agreeable emotional state is almost a reversion to the infantile in its intensity and may even be pursued by 'playing baby'. For most Europeans, indulgences of that variety are left behind in infancy, by rigorous suppression by both peers and adults. The Japanese encourage and amplify this phenomenon to create and sustain an emotion, *amae*, quite distinct from anything to be found in the adult repertoire of Western cultures. John McDoe (personal communication) has suggested that something like *amae* may be on the the the rise in the West with the recent emphasis on 'mothering wives'. Perhaps the 'tired businessman' who allows himself to be petted and cosetted at home is experiencing something like Japanese *amae* (see Morsbach, 1976).

3   A strong form exists in one culture of that which is weak in another: Most of us feel uncomfortable when we see someone, even a stranger, behaving foolishly, rudely, or otherwise badly. Spaniards feel this emotion especially acutely, so acutely that it is treated as a distinct emotion, '*verguenza ajena*' (perhaps: 'alien' or 'alienating shame'). Eduardo Crespo, reports from Madrid that television programs showing someone behaving badly can be almost unbearable to a Spaniard, due to the force of *verguenza ajena*. There is a well-known Iberian cultural complex into which this seems to fit, namely the cluster of customs and concepts built around the notion of *dignidad*.

4   There may also be historical changes in the emotional repertoire of a continuous national culture. In the psychological literature of the Middle Ages and early Renaissance, long discussions of the emotion 'accidie' are particularly prominent. The history of accidie (Latin *acedia*) is closely bound up with changing conceptions of religious duty. The emotion is first reported under the nickname 'the noonday demon' by Evragius, in Alexandrian times. Hermits who found it difficult to keep up their devotions through boredom were victims of it. But the boredom was not touched with guilt or shame. Rather it was qualified by despair and sadness, the gloom that comes over one who has lost the warmth of God's regard. *Acedia* was associated with *tristicia*. Accidie disappears from the

explicit repertoire of English emotions with the rise of Protestantism, and its disappearance seems to be accompanied by a more explicit relation between dereliction of duty in general, and the twin emotions guilt and shame. The cure of accidie involves more than the more resumption of the abandoned task. It must be taken up again joyfully.

5 My final category of culturally distinctive psychological phenomena are those I think should be called 'quasi-emotions'. These are felt states of being that are closely related to the physical conditions of life. The misery one feels when coming down with 'flu, and struggling home through a cold rainy night, is a particularly disagreeable quasi-emotion. But, to turn to the bright side, I propose to concentrate on the more agreeable winter feelings. Take the case of 'cosiness'. We say we feel cosy, that a particular sort of occasion or physical environment is cosy, and so on. I call 'cosiness' a quasi-emotion also partly because of its double meaning as a feeling and as a description of place. (The word may come from the Gaelic *cosh*, a small hole into which one might crawl and so be snug.) The interest of this quasi-emotion is heightened by the fact that in some other European languages words for similar but not identical states of being exist. There seems to be a marked absence of such terminology from Mediterranean languages. The Dutch word *gezellig* refers to a state experienced in somewhat similar circumstances to those in which we would use the word 'cosy'. However, my Dutch informants assure me that one could not be *gezellig* alone. (This Dutch word derives from the word for friend.) Thus the Dutch word picks out a quasi-emotion somewhere between the English 'cosy' and German '*gemütlich*'. The latter, I believe, is confined to companionable occasions. The Finns have the word *kodikas* from the word *koti* meaning home. (I am particularly indebted to L. Helkana for explaining *kodikas* to me.) While the word can be applied to rooms, ambiences, even people, it lacks the duality of cosy and *gezellig*, since it does not appear able to be used to refer to anything like a feeling, collective or individual.

These kinds of cases could be multiplied a hundredfold. There can be little doubt that even if there are some universal emotions, the bulk of mankind live within systems of thought and feeling that bear little but superficial resemblances to one another.

Individuals in a social order

Giddens (1984) coined the term 'structuration' to refer to the process by which persons are shaped by social forces and practices, and then in turn such persons shape society to reproduce at least similar versions of the practices which produced them. Structuration is the process by which the boundary between the social and the personal is crossed and recrossed.

The Vygotsky cycle

In the introduction to this chapter, I suggested that it was helpful to look on the array of persons as a 'space'. Each person is a point-like place at which are located the speech-acts that go to make up the conversations of mankind. Speech-acts are the social forces of the actual utterances and hearings by speakers and listeners. The world to which psychology, and particularly social psychology, should be directing its research is just this clamor of conversation. The account of emotions and of the 'inner self' that was set out above is based on the idea that the personal psychology of each individual is created by the appropriation of various conversational forms and strategies from that discourse. Insofar as individual people construct a personal discourse on the model of public discourse, they become complex 'mental' beings with unique 'inner worlds'. Even as very young children, human beings soon cease to be the locations for those simple utterances that are truly the unstudied contributions of the naive, unselfconscious speaker to the public conversation. To develop concepts for making the most of this insight (which history must surely ascribe to L. S. Vygotsky) and to mark off the social constructionist approach from Cartesianism, I reproduce in figure 1 a psychological 'space' I have advocated in other places (Harré 1983). The axis of MANI-FESTATION expresses a dimension that marks the distinction between overt and public displays of some emotional state, intellectual activity and so on, and the ways we can keep at least some of these matters to ourselves, by 'keeping our cards close to our chests'. For instance, if one finds oneself in conversation with someone whose opinions are not only strongly held but contrary to one's own, one can keep one's disapproval private in the interests of public amity – perhaps motivated by an obligation to one's host and hostess not to cause a scene. The distinction between public manifestation and private seclusion of psychological states and processes is more general than the Cartesian distinctions of 'inner' and 'outer' or 'subjective' and 'objective'. (See Sabini and Silver,

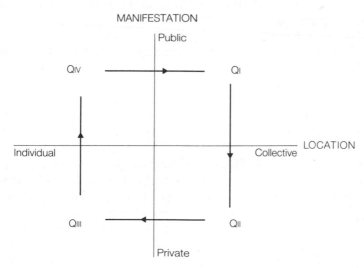

MANIFESTATION

Figure 1   Vygotsky 'space'

1982, for an excellent analysis of the muddles that lie behind the fusion of those classical distinctions in the most common form of Cartesianism.) The unconscious becomes anything that cannot be brought out into public conversation.

The second dimension of the Vygotskyean 2-space lies along a continuum between individual and collective realizations of psychological phenomena. For example, rationality could be a logical constraint on the thought-processes of individual thinkers. But research has shown it to be more useful to think of rationality as a property of conversation and to think of its sources in certain social conventions governing the style of speech and writing of the occupants of different public roles. (See Latour and Woolgar, 1979.) Moral reasoning generally seems to take place in a conclave rather than in the soliloquies of solitary individuals.

Two orthogonal dimensions engender a two-dimensional 'space' with four quadrants. I label these as in figure 1. Quadrant I is the social world, while Quadrant III is the personal realm. I shall call this a 'Vygotsky space'. It can be used in at least two different ways. One is in the definition of the basic project of developmental psychology. According to the constructionist viewpoint, 'development' must occur through the transfer of the rules and conventions that govern public conversation and other social practices from Quadrant I, via Quadrant II, to Quadrant III. In general, there is a natural priority to Quadrant I, the social or public-collective quadrant.

Vygotsky (1962, 1978) was among the first to study the ways the acquisition of the forms of public language shaped individual minds. Development just is the step-wise acquisition of language, for it is in this acquisition that the ordered structure of mind is brought about. The first step is the privatization of the language of the local social group, as the child picks up the trick of conducting its thinking in private. Piaget mistakenly thought that the use of self-referential expressions to preface much infant speech was a sign of egocentricity, the occupancy of a self-centred view of the world which precluded the taking up of the standpoint of another person. By the 1930s, Vygotsky had shown this idea to be mistaken. 'Egocentric' speech disappears at a certain age not because the child has come to be able to take the point of view of another person, but because the '*cogito*', by which, as Kant remarked, all my thoughts are introduced as mine, has become the unattended and redundant mark of *sotto voce* soliloquy. In a series of quite brilliant empirical demonstrations, Margaret Donaldson (1978) has conclusively shown that, if the request is put in terms appropriate to the situation, even very young children have no difficulty in working out how the world might look from the point of view of another observer, and even how one's moral perspective might depend on the group to which one belonged (see Linaza, 1985).

Later, there is a further development by which the 'space' I have labelled Quadrant III comes to be filled out with all sorts of highly individualized thought and feeling, plans and intentions, most of which will never be produced in the public realm of Quadrant IV. I believe the study of the psychology of such tropes as metaphor and of such cognitive processes as analogical reasoning and judgment will throw much light on the transition from Quadrant II to Quadrant III.

Finally, we must take account of the way individual innovations are published and returned to social 'space' again, the 'space' of Quadrant IV. Jokes, poems, new social practices, individual ways of dressing, may all fall flat when produced in public. Some of our innovations may be taken up by the community and transferred to Quadrant I when they become part of the collective practices of the culture. It is these we call 'creative'.

Psychological symbiosis

The 'Vygotsky space' helps to describe the dynamics of the acquisition of an ordered mind by an individual embedded within a linguistic community with its own distinctive moral order. But it offers no theory of how individual patterns of thought are shaped by social practices. An important aspect of this process is a relationship I, following Shotter (1984), call 'psychological symbiosis'. Analysis of the ways mothers speak to and for their infants reveals that most mothers address their children as if the babies had well-developed psychological resources and skills. Babies are ascribed intentions, wants, powers of reason and even of moral judgment, and it is to these ascriptions rather than to the baby's own behavior that the mother reacts. To adapt a schema I have used before, we can represent the changing patterns of psychological symbiosis diagramatically in figure 2. The relative sizes of the mother symbol and the infant symbol represent the extent to which individual responsibility for some psychological or moral trait taken (by the mother) as belonging to the infant actually is rooted in the competence and knowledge of the one or the other.

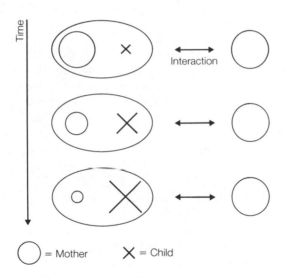

Figure 2   Psychological symbiosis

The contributions of the mother (and others among the child's intimates) complement the activities of the child, in order to present the child as an intellectually and morally mature person. In short, children always *appear as persons* within those communities where psychological symbiosis is practised, notably the family circle.

What happens during the developmental process thus conceived? In one of his many differences from Piaget, Vygotsky suggested that step-wise advances in competence, with nth being a prerequisite for the accomplishment of the $(n+1)$th must be preceded by certain specific preparatory experiences in the 'zone of proximal development'. Psychological symbiosis suggests very precise hypotheses about what those experiences must be. But what corresponds to Piaget's 'assimilation/accommodation'? One hypothesis that has economy to recommend it is that children merely imitate bits and pieces of the complementary activities of the symbiotic other, by which that other completes the performance of the dyad, the notional person of whom the infant is but one component. In this way, and in no particular order, the junior member of various symbiotic dyads builds up a mere aggregate of fragments. It may be that like many organic processes such as the forming the three-dimensional structures of large organic molecules, once all the components are there the structure forms naturally and necessarily without any further mysterious synthetic process, and requires no template.

The dyadic relation of psychological symbiosis is a conversational space. If all conversation spaces are structured by locally valid systems of role-related obligations, rights and duties, symbiotic dyads should also be so structured. So the 'imitation' story must be supplemented by attention to the differential rights and obligations to display social skills, rationality of judgment, moral maturity and so on. One would expect that at different stages in the life history of a symbiotic dyad changing distributions of rights and duties would devolve upon the junior and the senior member of this or that dyad. Furthermore, cultures should be expected to differ in the way those rights are distributed, at different ages, with respect to mother, father, grandmother, teacher, sibling and so on.

Given the extent to which the honor and reputation of someone is wrapped in their character, their presumed psychological nature, and so on, it would not be surprising if the phenomenon of psychological symbiosis were to be found amongst the close-knit clusters of people. I have seen it develop between supervisors and their graduate students, husbands and wives, doctors and patients, and have even seen it become pathological – as in a case where a parent almost always answers the questions addressed to a grown-up but by now highly dependent and psychologically maimed daughter. J. S. Bruner has spoken of the mother's 'theory' of how and what the child ought to be. He has seen the process at work in the way mother–infant interactions develop. This idea, too, should be generalized. A fascinating research area opens here, since so very little is known of the person theories held by the members of any society.

Enriching the research paradigm

But the Vygotsky space can also be used to organize research into the psychology of mature people. Many common terms for psychological states and processes refer as much to the phenomena of the public-collective realm as to individual-private subjective states and cognitive processes. For example, 'reasoning' refers both to certain communal conversational forms ('brainstorming', 'kicking an idea round') and to private and individual cognitive processes. Moral reasoning sometimes takes the form of a private conversation, a juxtaposition of pros and cons, but sometimes and more usually it occurs in a discussion among two or more people. As Sabini and Silver (1982) have argued, it may take place 'off stage' so to speak, during gossip. Social constructionism holds that private cognitive processes that might be called reasoning are modeled on (because they are derived from) certain communal practices we could also reasonably call 'coming to a reasoned decision'. By the same token, individual efforts at moral reasoning are best thought of as simulacra of those kinds of public discourse in the course of which communal decisions emerge.

The most important feature common to all four realms is language. Language is both a public and private medium of thought and social action. It has the capacity and flexibility to expand and to develop new forms that are at first unique to individuals but can return to the public domain as contributions to an ever-changing conversation. But language is not the only medium common to all four quadrants. There are many other symbolic systems stabilized by communal conventions and also taken up by individuals as a medium for private, individual thought. I have in mind such media as music and the other arts. Various images such as models and diagrams as well as works of art have the necessary duality.

The Cartesian scheme sharply polarized the ontology of psychology into entities proper to an inner-subjective world and entities available to the scrutiny of anyone in the public-objective domain. If 'mind' is the totality of all that is inner and subjective, it is a complete mystery how the mind of another could be known to us. At best, we would be dependent on a hazardous 'decoding' of physical behavior. But the Vygotskyean space allows us to think of the mind of another person as spread over all four quadrants. The mind of a painter inventing and displaying new images is perhaps more amply developed in Quadrants II and IV, while the mind of a bureaucrat tied to the most routine of societal norms mainly inhabits Quadrants I and II.

Consider briefly and finally the case of research into memory. The Cartesian schema provides the researcher with a two-phase project. Individual recollection is the cognitive process; ontologically, this refers to a private, subjective upshot, the memorial moment in which, in one of various formats, a representation of a past event is experienced. Research consists in studying these memorial moments through their public representation in speaking, writing, marking charts and so on. This is all very well in its way. But if understanding human life is the final goal of the enterprise, this kind of research is only the beginning. How is the performative operator 'I remember that . . .' actually used? Even unstructured casual observation shows that not all recollections issue in declarations that are accepted by the community. 'I remember that . . .' is to claim; and, like all claims, it is in need of justification. The Vygotsky space permits a more complex three-phase process to be envisaged. The fact that recollections, particularly of events in early childhood, and memorial offerings as evidence in legal trials, are usually subjected to public negotiation shows that the process of assimilation into the conversation of the public-collective Quadrant I needs to be included in our picture of the process of remembering. Checking a past event against a present recollection is logically impossible, and checking a recollection against present traces of a past event is both difficult for lack of record and problematic by reason of the in-principle revisability of all inductive inferences. In real life, a social process is set in motion, by which claims and counterclaims about accurate recollections are registered; often, the settlement of disputes seems to be achieved by the exercise of memorial rights vested in some role-holder – for example, in family discusions, this often seems to be the mother. So the role of Quadrant I is easily confirmed, even where private mental life is usually supposed to reign supreme.

REFERENCES

Aristotle, *Rhetoric*, 1378a, 30–2.
Austin, J. L. 1962: *How to Do Things with Words*. New York: Oxford University Press.
Averill, J. R. 1982: *Anger and Aggression: an essay on emotion*. New York; Springer Verlag.

Donaldson, M. 1978: *Children's Minds*. London: Croom Helm.

Duval, S. and Wicklund, R. A. 1972: *A Theory of Objective Self-awareness*. New York: Academic Press.

Giddens, A. 1984: *The Constitution of Society*. Cambridge: Polity Press.

Harré, R. 1979: *Social Being*. Oxford: Basil Blackwell.

Harré, R. 1983: *Personal Being*. Oxford: Basil Blackwell.

Latour, B. and Woolgar, S. 1979: *Laboratory Life*. Los Angeles: Sage.

Leventhal, H. 1980: Towards a comprehensive theory of emotions. Advances in Experimental Social Psychology, 13, 139–207.

Linaza, J. 1985: The game of marbles. *Oxford Review of Education*, 10, 67–70

Lutz, C. 1985: Goals, event and understanding in Ifaluk emotion theory. In N. Quinn and D. Holland (eds), *Cutural Models in Language and Thought*. Cambridge: Cambridge University Press.

Mead, G. H. 1934: *Mind, Self and Society*. Chicago: University of Chicago Press.

Morsbach, H. 1976; Some Japanese-Western linguistic differences: the case of '*amae*'. In R. Harré (ed.), *Life Sentences*, Chichester: John Wiley.

Plutchik, R. 1980: A general psychoevolutionary theory of emotion. In R. Plutchik and H. Kellerman, *Emotion Theory, Research and Experience*, New York: Academic Press.

Sabini, J. and Silver, M. 1982: *Moralities of Everyday Life*. New York: Oxford University Press.

Sapir, E. 1957: *Culture, Language and Personality*, edited by D. G. Mandelbaum, Berkeley and Los Angeles: University of California Press.

Schachter, S. 1971: *Emotion, Obesity and Crime*. New York: Academic Press.

Searle, J. R. 1984: Minds, Brains and Science. London: BBC Publications.

Shotter, J. 1984: *Social Accountability and Selfhood*. Oxford: Basil Blackwell.

Strawson, Sir P. F. 1959: *Individuals*. London: Methuen.

Vygotsky, L. S. 1962: *Thought and Language*. Cambridge Mass.: MIT Press.

Vygotsky, L. S. 1978: *Mind in Society*. Cambrdge, Mass. and London: Harvard University Press.

Warner, C. T. 1986: Anger and similar delusions. In R. Harré (ed.), *The Social Construction of Emotions*, Oxford: Basil Blackwell.

Wittgenstein, L. 1953: *Philosophical Investigation*. Oxford: Basil Blackwell.

Wood, L. 1983: Loneliness. In R. Harré and R. Lamb (eds), *The Encyclopedic Dictionary of Psychology*, Oxford: Basil Blackwell.

5

Social Psychology as a Science

Paul F. Secord

As is clear from this book, psychology is currently undergoing an intensive re-examination. Changing views in the philosophy of science are generating questions about the very foundations of psychology, about its deepest assumptions and its status as a science, and about its relation to the natural sciences on the one hand and to the social sciences on the other. At the same time, tension between psychology as a laboratory science and those areas of psychology that attempt to deal with more human concerns continues to produce critiques within the discipline itself.

Under these circumstances it seems appropriate to examine intensively a field of psychology that has always been rather separate from general psychology – social psychology. Throughout the twentieth century, this subdiscipline, although influenced by its parent discipline has increasingly moved toward the status of an independent field. Moreover, social psychology has a peculiar status, compared with most other subdisciplines of psychology. Most subdisciplines of psychology are relatively independent of other disciplines, but a few are not. Just as neuropsychology has a close affinity with neurobiology, social psychology has – at least in principle – a close affinity with the social sciences, especially sociology.

As will be shown, however, this affinity has obtained more in principle than in practice. A separate and very different social psychology has developed within sociology itself, and psychological social psychology has been very little influenced by it. Each discipline has, for the most part, published its own journals and textbooks, and in many universities and colleges each of the departments offers social psychology independently of the other. This separate state of affairs appears to have been brought about by the different natures of the two parent disciplines as well as by their different attitudes toward the philosophy of science, and this chapter will identify the features of these disparate orientations. Moreover, lest one think that, as the decades go by, these subdisciplines would eventually discover what is of merit in their opposite number and modify their own subdiscipline so as to take into account relevant features – and thereby produce some coalescence – in fact only isolated instances of rapprochement have occurred. In my view, the two fields are on the whole no closer today than they were in the late 1940s, when I was a graduate student.

Three polarities

This chapter is written around three polarities, each of which describes characteristics expressed differently in the two parent disciplines, that have shaped their social psychologies. The first polarity, *positivistic versus humanistic science*, shows how the different views of science, implicit or occasionally explicit in psychology or sociology, have produced different modes of thinking and operating. Much more than sociology, psychology has been influenced by the standard view of science, patterned after what the physical sciences seemed to be. Although the functionalist movement in sociology likewise follows a similar template, other approaches take into account features more distinctive of humans – particularly language. Understanding the differences is important, for now that philosophical views of psychology and the social sciences are undergoing a thorough upheaval, the possibility arises, for the first time, of a real rapprochement between the two social psychologies.

A second polarity having important ramifications for the two social psychologies contrasts a *focus on the individual with focus on society*. Psychologists deeply believe that a focus on individuals can provide full explanations of behavior that are not dependent on extra-psychological considerations, and that historical circumstances and social context can somehow be circumvented, perhaps by transforming and representing them in psychological terms. Thus, the laboratory experiment reigns as a principal method, and the behavior of individuals is central. Associated with this stance is a strong methodological individualism (in contrast to holism); even institutional behavior can be explained in terms of the behavior of each of the separate individuals.

As might be expected, most sociologists take a radically opposed position. Many sociologists vehemently oppose any attempt to 'psychologize' sociological explanations. For some, who emphasize Durkheim's 'social facts', social phenomena are to be explained without reference to individual behavior or the use of any psychological principles. Clearly, sociologists, too, subscribe to autonomy, but in this instance, to the autonomy of sociological explanation.

A third polarity, closely related to the second, contrasts the *'inner' with the 'outer'*. Psychology has long been preoccupied with 'inner' structures and processes, despite its involvement with behaviorism. Behaviorism never really succeeded in escaping from this orientation; behaviorists found it necessary to smuggle mental concepts back in. And certainly during the past two decades, behaviorism has faded and cognitive science has surged into the foreground. Along with it has come a renewed focus on inner processes. From one perspective, this preoccupation with the mental might seem to be quite natural; after all, isn't psychology about the mind? Isn't its purpose to explain what's going on in people's heads and how it leads them to behave in particular ways? The opposite view, characterizing much of sociology, emphasizes the situated, culture-bound, language-impregnated, historical nature of human action and suggests that we must look outside of the individual if we are to understand human behavior.

In what follows, the two social psychologies will be examined for features that relate to each of the several polarities sketched above. Although this is not the place for a history of the two social psychologies, historical highlights will be alluded to when they can be seen from these polarities. At the same time, other features bearing on current discussions and related to the polarities remarked also deserve to be considered.

A caveat is essential here. The purpose of this discussion is critical: the limits of the two approaches are featured, and noticeably less attention is given to the strengths of each. My intention is not destructive; it is not to imply that either approach is worthless. Despite limitations, each has been productive, and the methods of each seem reasonable. Our end goal is to identify the salient reqirements of a social psychology capable of adequately explaining social behavior and free of the limitations of prevailing views.

The standard view of science

The standard or received view of science is well known and is described in detail in many sources (Brown, 1977; Scheffler, 1967; Suppe, 1977).

Here it will only be briefly outlined. The limitations of the standard view can be seen more clearly when it is compared with a more contemporary perspective, so the description of each of its features given below is followed by parenthetical comments that show by contrast a more contemporary view. In the standard view:

1 The source of knowledge is empirical; theory and data are sharply distinguished. Data are the foundation for all knowledge; hypotheses are tested against the data. Data are regarded as independent of theory; and the validity of theory depends on its 'correspondence' with data. Knowledge of phenomena that are not directly observable is possible only if theoretical statements pertaining to phenomena can be verified. (Most philosophers of science nowadays depart from this standard view and emphasize that data are always theory-dependent; observations are typically made only from the standpoint of some theoretical position. Two observations of the 'same' phenomenon made from different theoretical perspectives may or are likely to yield different data. Thus, what social scientists often regard as 'facts' are nothing of the kind; they are theory-loaded observations. As an example, reflect upon the radical behaviorist's observation of a 'stimulus' or a 'response'.)

2 Strict constraints are put on the form that theories can take. Theoretical terms are hypothetical constructs and gain their meaning through systematic relations with other terms in the theory, or else by being connected to observations by correspondence rules or operational definitions. Additional meanings are 'surplus' and are not allowed. (Contemporary philosophy of science, influenced by intensive historical examination of how scientists actually work, views theory more as a set of working propositions that may contain concepts far removed from observation. Theories are not refuted or confirmed; they function as a rationale or framework for research investigations. The real measure of a theory's worth is the extent to which it expands our knowledge of reality.)

3 Given the low status of theory and the stringent constraints on its formation, research tends to be atheoretical, and is concerned primarily with testing hypotheses related to variables closely tied to observations. (From a philosophical perspective, to the extent that scientists actually work in the above fashion, only relatively trivial, non-generalizable knowledge is apt to be gained. More elaborate theory is required if science is to have any power. Suppe (1977,

p. 726) notes, for example, that, as scientific theory becomes more and more sophisticated, 'the interpretive aspects of observations become increasingly more subtle, theoretical, and removed from what we directly perceive.' By virtue of this theoretical power, he continues, it becomes possible to establish important principles by performing only a small number of experiments or observations. It follows that modern physics has never reflected the standard view of science, although it seems evident that many psychologists and social scientists have worked along lines depicted by the standard view.)

4   Conceptions of causality follow a Humean view: causal relations are regular contingent relations between events. When strict regularity cannot be achieved, relations between independent and dependent variables or probabilistic relations between sets of variables are the goal. Following Hempel (1963), explanation is subsumption under a general law. An exceptionless ideal is never achieved, and in practice explanations are inferred from rela-tionships discovered to hold between independent and dependent variables. (There is little consensus in contemporary philosophy of science on views that would replace these ideas of causality and explanation. Still, scientific *theories* do explain phenomena. Also, given the generally acknowledged defects of the standard view, freeing theory from its constraints can only improve the prospects for adequate explanations as well as clarify causal thinking.)

Philosophy of science emerged largely in relation to the work of the physical scientists, and thus represents a particular kind of science. Quite possibly, that is the only kind of science, although the alternative argument is that human society and human nature can be the subject matter of a quite different kind of science. Still another position is that the natural sciences have been badly misrepresented in philosophy's standard view of science, and that the natural sciences may well have parallels to the human sciences when properly conceived (see Bhaskar, 1975, 1978, 1979; Harré, 1970; Margolis, this book).

The standard view and the social psychologies

In the remainder of the discussion, psychological social psychology will be abbreviated PSP and sociological social psychology, SSP, and the representatives of these disciplines will be referred to as PSPs and SSPs, respectively.

Psychological social psychology (PSP)

Historians of psychology would all agree, it seems clear, that the standard view of science was implicit (and sometimes explicit) in the work of psychologists. Moreover, as a discipline anxious to establish its status as an independent science, its practitioners went out of their way to demonstrate how (and that) its theories and procedures could achieve an admissable level of rigor. Quite naturally, their explications conformed to what seemed salient in the most acceptable science of the day. Many psychology books were noted for the excessive space devoted to describing investigative procedures while giving short shrift to actual findings.

In general psychology, following the standard view means that individual behaviors are reduced to one or more 'dependent variables', variables measured by observing the behavior of persons. Human action in all its richness is narrowed to the smallest possible focus, typically one or more nonlinguistic acts that can be quantified. The dependent variables are seen as a function of a set of 'independent variables', which are also specified as narrowly as possible. These typically are conditions specified by the experimenter, and are usually produced through some form of manipulation of the participants in the experiment. Operations and measurements are primarily physicalistic, so that they can be performed by any trained observer. Just as a machine functions in a certain way under certain conditions, persons behave according to their present physical and psychological states and the stimulus situation. Prediction and control are emphasized and, as in physics, the experimental method is the scientific ideal.

Given a strong commitment to this view of science, psychological specialties that lent themselves to the experimental method achieved the highest status and prestige in the eyes of psychologists. Moreover, the greater the success in breaking down a complex behavior into sharply defined variables and the greater the rigor of the operations used to measure them, the more the research was respected. All too often, however, this was accomplished by doing research with animals instead of humans or, if working with humans, by structuring the experiment so that the use of language was impossible and the laboratory situation was reduced to the simplest possible terms.

Social psychology initially was characterized as both 'applied' and 'soft'. If PSP was to become really respectable, it was thought, it must become an experimental science and must achieve greater rigor of definition and measurement. General psychology developed an ever more sophisticated experimental methodology and an elaborate array of powerful statistical procedures, and PSP had to adopt these methods if it was to be respected. This is exactly what happened. Techniques adopted included complex methodologies for assigning subjects to treatment and control groups, factorial designs, and analysis of variance and covariance. Non-experimental studies applied equally sophisticated techniques, such as stepwise multiple regression, canonical correlation, and path analysis. All of these applications more or less required the reduction of social behavior to precisely defined variables.

Even in its earliest beginnings, experiments were not unknown in social psychology. For example, just prior to the twentieth century, Triplett (1897) had observed from official records that the maximum speed of bicycle riders was about 20 per cent greater when paced by a visible cycle. Wondering whether productivity in general could be increased through aggregative performance as contrasted with performing alone, Triplett did an experiment in which children wound fishing reels, either alone or together, and obtained a result similar to that found in bicycle riding. This pioneer experiment on 'social facilitation' among co-acting individuals was followed by others in the attempt to establish the conditions for social facilitation.

Although scattered experiments in social psychology continued to appear in subsequent years, it was not until Kurt Lewin introduced 'group dynamics' that the experiment came into its own. One of his most important contributions was to demonstrate that various group structures and processes could be studied in the laboratory. Perhaps the best-known of all of the studies of this movement is the Lewin, Lippitt, and White (1939) research on group climate or atmosphere, in which the experimenters set up democratic, *laissez-faire*, and authoritarian group structures in laboratory settings and measured their effects on productive tasks. This pioneer effort led to many follow-up experiments on leadership styles, and more generally, the group dynamics movement produced a wide variety of experiments on other topics.

During the enormous growth of higher education following World War II, experimentation rapidly became the method of choice of PSP, culminating in the founding, in 1965, of the prestigious Society for Experimental Social Psychology. The consequence was that topics chosen for investigation were those that lent themselves to laboratory experimentation, while other topics that could not be studied in the laboratory were less intensively studied or even ignored. Social psychologists pursuing experimental programs of research generally received the greatest recognition, and much less attention was paid to the rare investigator who studied non-experimental topics.

At the same time it is worth noting that this rich, productive period stressing experimentation was for about two decades primarily concerned with studies of group processes that went beyond the individual. It was Lewin's genius to show that group phenomena that transcend individual behaviors could be investigated in the laboratory (as well as in field situations) and to lead the way for social psychologists to think about group phenomena (in contrast to individual phenomena) in theoretical terms.

The early post-World War II period was extraordinarily productive in generating numerous experimental studies of small group processes. Thus, in their widely adopted social psychology textbook, Secord and Backman (1964) devoted seven chapters to small group processes, on such topics as interpersonal attraction, social power, status and communication, social norms and conformity, leadership, group productivity and satisfaction, and intergroup relations. Although some of these processes (for example, attraction, status) can be discussed apart from group settings, these seven chapters demonstrated their extensive involvement in group dynamics. During the period in question, from mid-century to the late 1960s, experimentation on small-group behavior remained a dominant theme in PSP. As will be seen in a later section, however, this interest in group behavior faded, and was replaced by orientations that stressed individual behavior and inner or mental processes.

Sociological social psychology (SSP)

Whether one looks at general psychology and general sociology, or, more specifically, at PSP and SSP, it is clear that sociology has been much less influenced than psychology by the positivist view of science. It would seem that the standard view of science was not adopted because, given their interest in societal processes, sociologists could hardly escape confrontation with language, culture and large-scale social processes, and presumably the standard view did not adapt well to the study of such phenomena. For one thing, *social theory* has always been considered a respectable specialty for a sociologist to have, but in psychology, being a theorist elicits the 'armchair' epithet from one's colleagues. At least some sociological theory is highly abstract and far removed from any data source, and thus is outside of the positivist framework.

Although a few sociologists used experimental methods to study small-group behavior, experimentation was never very popular, and sociologists were often very critical of the conclusions drawn by experimental social psychologists and the methods by which they arrived at them. Thus the central method of the positivists plays only a minor role in sociology.

Some forms of macrosociology, however, adopted a positivist framework. Emile Durkheim (1895) set the pattern for this kind of sociology. Emphasis is upon *social facts* as apart from and abstracted from individual behavior. Often these are represented by frequencies or rates of various kind of acts, and much of this work today falls under the heading of demography. Thus, suicide rates, rates for various types of crimes, for marriage and divorce, births, deaths, educational attainment and the like constitute social facts. These statistics are ascribed a significance apart from individual actions, and the sociological effort is to relate them to other social facts, as in Durkheim's famous observations relating suicide to anomie in a society. Moreover, these social facts are treated in terms of mathematical models or other sophisticated statistical procedures: the level of abstraction and formality fits well into the positivist framework.

A dominant theme in sociology during the post-World War II period was structural-functionalism, perhaps best represented by the work of Talcott Parsons and Robert K. Merton. In some, but not all, respects their work had a positivist flavor. Central to Parsons's thinking was the idea of the social system, a structural interpretation of how human behavior is organized. Social systems were characterized by Parsons (1951) in terms of interacting social roles. An institution, for example, was depicted as a set of positions or statuses, toward which its members had sets of expectations as to how the occupants of the positions should behave. By discovering the expectations held for the positions, examining their consistency or their conflicting nature, and observing how the roles were enacted, the sociological investigator could gain greater understanding of how the institution functioned. This sort of sociological theory does not fit too well with positivism, for many aspects of it are subjective in nature and too far removed from observation. But Parsons and especially Merton did emphasize objectivity and rigor in measurement and in the formulation of concepts.

Structural-functionalism is the view that sociological phenomena are structured (that is patterned and repetitive behaviors) and can be subjected to functional analysis. Although subjective dispositions such as motives and purposes may be assumed to underlie the relevant behaviors the emphasis is on the objective consequences of the patterned actions in question. What are their consequences? Are they functional or dysfunctional? What sorts of constraints are operating and through what mechanisms are the functions fulfilled? Merton's prodigious output covered such topics as manifest and latent functions operating in society, sociological theory and its relation to empirical research, social structure and anomie, bureaucratic structure and personality, reference group behavior, the sociology of knowledge, and many other topics.

Within sociology, three distinct social psychologies can be identified. Some of the work in the structuralist-functional tradition can be considered to be social psychological. This form of SSP has a somewhat diffuse identity, in that its practitioners often merely think of themselves as sociologists rather than social psychologists. House (1977) calls it *psychological sociology* and sees it as relating 'macrosocial phenomena (for example, organizations, societies and aspects of the social structures and processes thereof) to individuals' psychological attributes and behavior, usually using quantitative but non-experimental (often survey methods)' (pp. 161–2). Another topical name for it is *social structure and personality*. Thus, this kind of SSP at least loosely fits positivist constraints.

More visible SSPs were symbolic interactionism and, more recently, ethnomethodology. For both of these movements, the experimental method was anathema. Subjective methods of investigation were considered essential, and none of the positivist stipulations was considered relevant. These two forms of SSP will be described in a later section dealing with inner-outer polarities.

Social psychology and the individual/social polarity

Perhaps the best explanation of how PSP and SSP came to be so different from each other is a historical one: psychology has roots going back for centuries and is, by tradition and by definition, the study of the individual, which has ordinarily meant the mind. In contrast, sociology arose in the attempt to explain societal phenomena, such as the behavior of collections of people, the actions of groups, organizations and whole societies. PSP and SSP, respectively, emerged from these parent disciplines and for the most part adopted the polarized orientation appropriate to each parent discipline.

Except for the hiatus produced by the emergence of behaviorism, psychology has always been the study of individual minds and, even if behaviorism did not focus on the mind, the individual remained the center of attention. As will be seen in the final section, however, the question arises as to whether psychology can indeed remain autonomous in this sense. (See also the other chapters in this book for perspectives on the autonomy of psychology.)

Focus on the individual person was present in the early beginnings of twentieth centuury PSP. The strong individual bent of social psychologists is illustrated, for example, in Floyd Allport's (1924) *Social Psychology*. He reacted strongly to William McDougall's introduction of the concept of group mind, a term intended to recognize that, collectively, members of a group may share ideas, motives and habits that are not dependent on the ideas, motives and habits of any particular individual. Allport states:

> There is no psychology of groups which is not essentially and entirely a psychology of individuals. Social psychology must not be placed in contradistinction to the psychology of the individual; *it is a part of the psychology of the individual*, whose behavior it studies in relation to that sector of his environment comprised by his fellows. His biological needs are the ends toward which his social behavior is a developed means. *Within his organism are provided all the mechanisms by which social behavior is explained.* (p. 4, italics added)

Allport drew a distinction between co-acting and face-to-face groups of individuals. Co-acting individuals are those who are not directly interacting with each other, but rather with some other stimulus situation, as in the case of an audience of individuals working side-by-side but not cooperatively on a common task. Allport's interest was in social facilitation, as illustrated, under certain circumstances, by facilitating productivity among co-acting individuals merely because they are co-acting. The focus is clear: to strip away complexities due to a differentiated and structured group concept that might transcend individuals, and to explain behavior in purely individual terms.

What is at issue relates intimately to the well-known, long-standing philosophical debate over methodological individualism and holism applied to history and the human sciences. The point of contention rests with the relative contributions to social science explanations of constructs regarding individual persons or societal aggregates or societal properties. At the extremes, the individualist argues either that social facts are non-existent or that they can be explained in terms of individual actions, while the holist holds that individuals can only be understood as social beings that transcend the ordinary notion of a person, and that social cannot be reduced to individual actions.

The individualist position has been well put by Watkins (1959):

> ... the ultimate constituents of the social world are individual people who act more or less appropriately in the light of their

dispositions and understanding of their situation. Every complex social situation, institution or event is a result of a particular configuration of individuals, their dispositions, situations, beliefs, and physical resources and environment. There may be unfinished or halfway explanations of large scale phenomena (say, inflation) in terms of other large scale phenomena (say, full employment) but we shall not have arrived at rock bottom explanations of such large scale phenomena until we have deduced an account of them from statements about the dispositions, beliefs, resources, and interrelations of individuals.

It seems evident that PSP is more or less aligned with the position quoted. Much work in PSP has focused on the relation of the *individual* to society. Thus, how the individual perceives other persons or other features of society has been the subject of innumerable investigations. In the immediate post-World War II period, the 'New Look' in perception produced a wave of experiments designed to show how individual characteristics such as values or even personality characteristics could produce modified perceptions of both physical and social objects. This was followed by considerable interest in how impressions of persons were formed, and how stereotyping of persons according to their categorical memberships took place. Focus on individual behaviors was also illustrated by attempts to explain behaviors in terms of such individual concepts as attitudes, needs, habits, self-concepts, social comparison processes, cognitive schemata and the like. In fact, the methodological individualist position is largely an argument for the autonomy of psychology. No attempt will be made here to resolve the debate, but shortly, in discussing SSP, the holist position will become clear, and in the final section it will be argued that an adequate social psychology cannot possibly adopt an individualist stance.

As already noted, PSP came closest to transcending the individual in its treatment of small group behavior, a topic that was popular in both PSP and SSP from its beginnings in the 1940s to the 1960s. But the vigorous emergence of cognitive psychology over the past two decades had its influence on PSP and, apparently, even on SSP, and has pushed research on group behavior far into the background.

Sociological social psychology

With few exceptions, one only need read a social psychologist trained in sociology to appreciate the vast difference in orientation between SSP and PSP. Representatives of SSP persistently focus on social interaction or on institutions and society. Even when they are looking at individuals, their orientation is toward how that individual participates in a social context.

Sociological orientations were from the start oriented toward society or at least toward larger units within it, even when the sociologists were social psychologists. Just after the turn of the century, Sumner (1906) wrote of folkways and mores. And in his *Human Nature and the Social Order*, Charles Cooley (1902) described the self as a social entity, intimately linked with the interactive network within which a person acts.

One distinctive difference between PSP and SSP that became especially apparent from the 1940s onward was that, although PSP was *almost* monolithic, SSP was split into different opposing camps. Several distinctive lines of thought can be readily identified. The work of George Herbert Mead, developed early in the century and posthumously published in the 1930s, emphasized language and communication in interpersonal settings. For Mead, the person was very much a social being, and language and meaning were indispensable to understanding persons and society. His theoretical stance became known as symbolic interactionism, and social psychologists who followed him have identified themselves in those terms. They were scornful of experimental methods and also of large-scale sociological research based upon statistical methods. (This orientation will be treated in more detail in the next section.)

Another group of representatives within SSP adopted the structuralist-functionalist position, described earlier. They emphasized social structures or systems in which institutions, for example, were construed as networks of interacting social roles. Social roles were thought of as positions within the system, each of which had associated with it sets of expectations regarding how persons in given positions should behave. Thus, SSP theorists sought to explain in terms of social roles many of those behaviors that PSP theorists associated with personality. After all, they observed, people do not behave consistently from situation to situation, but, instead, enact roles appropriate to the situation of the moment. This group includes the psychological sociologists – particularly with regard to their efforts to relate individual characteristics to features of the larger society, as for example in the changes produced by modernization.

Floyd Allport, given his determined effort to explain social phenomena entirely in terms of individual behaviors, could be assigned his opposite number among the sociologists, although few would have regarded themselves as social psychologists. In fact, they rather fiercely denounced any efforts to 'psychologize' sociology; for them, sociological explanations were quite complete in and of themselves, and they shunned any reference to individual behavior mechanisms of cognitive processes at any level. One sees this for example in the controversy over Durkheim's famous study of suicide. Durkheim explained suicide in terms of a societal condition called anomie, a form of social disorganization in which many individuals have only weak or no attachments to social groups, such as the family and the church. Those favoring a 'pure' sociological explanation argued that anomie provided an explanation of suicide in its own right, that nothing need be added of the psychology of the individuals who committed suicide. The opposing view held that such explanations were incomplete without mention of the victims's own account (see Douglas, 1967).

As might be expected, few sociologists who eschew psychological explanation are social psychologists. Most representatives of SSP use a combination of individual and group or interpersonal processes to construct explanations. The symbolic interactionists illustrate the pattern.

Social psychology and inner–outer polarities

Psychological social psychology

The inward orientation of PSP is marked early in its history by its prominent use of the concept of attitude. The term *attitude* refers to certain regularities of an individual's feelings, thoughts and predispositions to act toward some aspect of his or her environment. It was thought that by using well-designed measurement devices, an intensive assessment of the attitudes of individuals could be used to predict how they would behave. This conception firmly focuses explanation on individual minds.

The concept of attitude had its beginnings in the 1920s, when L. L. Thurstone (1928) published his classic work adapting psychophysical methods to the measurement of attitudes. A few years later, Rensis Likert (1932) introduced his simplified method of attitude measurement, and social psychologists set about developing attitude scales for measuring attitudes toward every conceivable 'social object'. By 1954, Gordon Allport declared *attitude* to be 'the most distinctive and indispensable concept in contemporary American social psychology'

(p. 43). To the present day, the concept retains its vitality as reflected in an appreciable amount of research that continues to be published.

Although it is true that attitude is a concept within SSP as well as PSP, it is less prominent in the former and is treated rather differently. For example, the concept of attitude was first introduced by Thomas and Znaniecki, in 1918, in their famous five volume study, *The Polish Peasant in Europe and America*. These two *sociologists* defined social psychology as the scientific study of attitudes. Their treatment of the concept, however, was quite different from that later favored in PSP. Immigrants could only be understood, they argued, by obtaining from them accounts of their own understanding of their native culture and that of their adopted country, and of the progressive changes that took place in their attitudes as they adapted to their new country. Thus, attitudes were expressed in the ordinary language accounts of the immigrants rather than in a technical idiom; moreover, in explanations of 'assimilation', for example, attitude and social context were intimately related. In contrast, the treatment of attitudes in PSP was strongly influenced by the psychometric tradition within psychology itself – a focus that has become more and more sophisticated to our own day.

The shift in general psychology toward an interest in cognitive processes has been clearly paralleled by a comparable movement in PSP. Interest in small group processes gradually dwindled, in favor of focusing on individuals and looking inward at their minds. Thus, in 1974, Ivan Steiner, a leader in small group research, published an article entitled, 'Whatever happened to the small group in social psychology?'

Fritz Heider's (1958) influential *The Psychology of Interpersonal Relations* set the conditions for the first major thrust toward cognitive psychology within PSP. Actually, his book addressed mental processes more than relationships: it attempted to explain relationships in terms of mental processes, and it focused on consistency and inconsistency among the mental elements representing relationships. Many prominent social psychologists were drawn to the topic, which eventuated in an ency-clopedic work entitled *Theories of Cognitive Consistency: A Sourcebook* (Abelson, Aronson, McGuire, et al. 1968).

At about the same time, a further thrust toward cognitive processes was launched with the publication of Leon Festinger's (1957) *A Theory of Cognitive Dissonance*. Festinger held that when circumstances led individuals to behave in a manner contrary to their attitudes, 'cognitive dissonance' resulted. Changing one's attitude relieved the dissonance. Festinger's seminal theory inspired many hundreds of experiments during the next two decades.

Enough has been said about PSP to establish clearly that its representatives have overwhelmingly focused on processes that may be referred to as mental, inner, or cognitive. At the same time, they were much less attentive to explanatory features that must be said to be located in the 'external' world. Except for piecemeal studies, even language had been neglected as a subject of investigation. The laboratory experiment and psychometric procedures focused on attitude measurement were hardly favorably disposed to accomodate complex social facts.

Sociological social psychology

By and large, few sociologists choose to explain social behavior in terms of mental processes alone. Most SSPs focus either on interactions among individuals or on interactions between individuals and society. Few give attention to individual psychological processes that are inward-oriented; in fact, many specifically argue that sociological explanations are not dependent on or reducible to psychological ones.

The two most distinctive forms of SSP are symbolic interactionism and ethnomethodology. The former is associated with the work of George Herbert Mead (1934), and the latter is a somewhat more diffuse movement that has emerged in the last two decades as a rebellion against mainstream sociology. Proponents of each approach see their social psychology as representing a new or different paradigm at odds with conventional sociology and as more or less self-contained.

These subdisciplines are sometimes collected under the rubric of 'phenomenological sociology'. Hence, it might appear that the symbolic interactionists and the ethnomethodologists explain social behavior in terms of individual, inner processes, but that impression would be false. In both, the focus of attention is on social interaction or relations between individuals. Indeed, both individuals and society are considered to be abstractions; only the ongoing, dynamic interaction process is real. In fact, as Knorr-Cetina (1981) has suggested, this orientation constitutes an alternative to both methodological individualism and holism: it might be called *methodological situationalism*.

Symbolic interactionism

Let us consider symbolic interactionism first. Herbert Blumer (1969), who is perhaps the foremost contemporary exponent of Mead's ideas, identifies three premises on which symbolic interactionism is founded:

1   Human beings act toward things on the basis of the meanings that
     the things have for them.
2   The meaning of such things is derived from, or arises out of, the
     social interaction that one has with one's fellows.
3   These meanings are handled in, and modified through, an inter-
     pretative process used by the person in dealing with the things he
     encounters.

The first premise taken by itself might easily suggest that
interactionists do indeed look at mental processes as a source of
explanation. But they reject an interpretation of meaning as 'arising
through a coalescence of psychological elements in the person' (p. 4).
This is the point of the second premiss, which asserts that meaning arises
out of the interaction of two or more people: meanings are social
products formed through the defining activities of interacting persons.
For example, if smoke arises in a crowded theater, if the tendency of an
individual to call out 'Fire!' affects the members of a social group
similarly, and if that tendency to act is itself controlled by such effects,
the word 'fire' may be said to function socially as a significant symbol. It
is the reflexive character of such symbols that creates mind and language.
The third premiss also has an interactive theme: 'the actor selects,
checks, suspends, regroups and transforms the meanings in the light of
the *situation* in which he is placed and the direction of his action' (p. 5,
italics added). Individuals do not react directly to the actions of others,
but rather to the meanings they attach to these acts. Interaction involves a
reflexive process of action in which the actors jointly construct a
situational context as well as generate the actions that occur within that
context.

The recommended method of investigation reflects this focus.
Symbolic interactionists argue that only by becoming a participant in the
activities under study can the social psychologist gain an understanding
of them. Scientists must interact with those who are the objects of study
over an appreciable period of time, and must familiarize themselves,
through such participation, with situationally generated meanings. The
scientist cannot be an outsider, cannot remain aloof from the world
observed. But the scientist's conception must, also, go beyond the
commonsense reflection of mere participants; it must fathom social
processes hidden from them, at some deeper level of social interaction.

Here, both individual and mental processes are viewed as abstractions.
Persons are social beings, and cannot exist outside of the society in which
they are immersed. A Robinson Crusoe who survived alone on an island,

from infancy, would not be a social animal, would not be human. Language, a self, and all that we mean by the concept of a person would be lacking. Similarly, mental processes are not inside the person; their locus is in social interaction. Consciousness, mind, selves and the physical and social worlds inhere in such interaction and are not fully separable from it.

Ethnomethodology

Ethnomethodology is a somewhat more diffuse SSP than symbolic interactionism. Its adherents sometimes do not recognize one another as authentic representatives of the approach; and some actually do not wish to be called ethnomethodologists. Nevertheless, it is possible to identify the main tenets of their approach – which are usually associated with Garfinkel's (1967) monograph. An important part of their intellectual ancestry is drawn from the work of Alfred Schutz (1962, 1964, 1966).

Ethnomethodologists share with symbolic interactionists the idea that the parties to an interaction act in terms of the meanings they attach to their own and each other's actions as well as to the situation which frames their interaction. These meanings cannot just be read off by an observer who does not have a thorough understanding of the objectives and intentions of the actors or the time and place of interaction. The observer must 'get inside' the situation and gain an understanding of the actors' accounts of what is going on. How this is done is indicated in what Mannheim – as reported by Garfinkel (1967, p. 78) – called the *documentary method*:

The method consists of treating an actual appearance as 'the document of', as 'pointing to', as 'standing on behalf of' a presupposed underlying pattern. Not only is the underlying pattern derived from its individual documentary evidence, but the individual documentary evidences, in their turn, are interpreted on the basis of 'what is known' about the underlying pattern. Each is used to elaborate the other.

The method applies equally well to everyday talk and to sociological observation. Individuals seldom say exactly what they mean; their actions need clarification. Thus lay persons in interaction and sociologists interacting as observers of participants must learn to identify the action that underlies appearances. It is easy to misunderstand what is required here. It is not just that the observer must discover what the participants are thinking and feeling – or must be able to put himself or herself in their place. Participants may be unaware of the relevance (to their actions) of particular background biographical, contextual and commonsense factors. The observer, then, must ultimately penetrate beyond the participants' perspectives and develop an interpretation (differing from theirs) by making explicit what tacit knowledge and background circumstances are 'taken for granted' and how they serve the interactions that occur.

In this, the ethnomethodologists share common ground with the symbolic interactionists. They part company, however, over their concept of *indexicality*, as Layder (1981) has emphasized. The term signifies the idea that the meanings of acts are always indexed to the situation in which they occur; moreover, these meanings are always problematic, because they are constructed anew for each episode or situation. Language itself, as in any conversation, is never straightforwardly transparent: it has a profoundly reflexive and dialectical character, and speakers must continually clarify and elaborate in context, in order to be understood. Action is a practical, even tacit, accomplishment of everyday living; ethnomethodology is the study of how, in this strongly contexted sense, actors accomplish their everyday performances. By contrast, although symbolic interactionists also emphasize that meanings are socially constructed, they are said to be shared, to exist in society and to be straightforwardly legible. For them, participants enter situations that often are familiar: they are in fact defined by the meanings participants share. For ethnomethodologists, every situation is problematic; each is virtually unique, in the sense that it requires substantial on-site construction of meanings in the very course of interaction.

Although ethnomethodologists are not always clear on this ontological point, they usually deny the existence of a social world; in that respect they are closer to methodological individualists than to holists. They concede only the concrete practical activities of everyday life. Because of their indexicality, these activities have no permanence and cannot be objectively grasped in the way that physical objects may be examined. Although ethnomethodologists often speak of rules as underlying social interaction, these are not the social norms of the symbolic interactionists and certainly not the structural norms associated with the theory of social roles in Parsonian sociology. These roles exist only in the single occasions of their supposed use; and that use is, as already remarked, decidedly problematic and inexplicit (Cicourel, 1969).

Ethnomethodologists are especially critical of sociological approaches that attempt to explain behavior at the level of social structure, and oppose both abstract theory and positivist methodologies. Their objection is primarily focused on attempts to explain human behavior in terms of abstract variables without ever connecting those variables to concrete situations – that is, wherever such variables spring from the mind of the investigator. Admittedly, investigators may be using their commonsense understanding of everyday life, but that connection is often not made explicit; moreover, the understanding of the investigator may be quite different from that of the various individuals under observation. For ethnomethodologists, every situation involves constructive work in which participants arrive at the meaning of a situation in the course of the action. This work, they complain, is never examined by positivist-oriented social scientists. Instead, the latter simply invent concepts and variables, using at best an incident or personal experience, but never systematically examine how the variables are situated in everyday life.

Implications from the several social psychologies

Macrostructures and social psychology

In both PSP and SSP, our ability to explain social behavior is limited by our failure to show how macrostructures bear on social interaction. Until recently macrostructures have been virtually ignored in PSP and, in SSP, both symbolic interactionism and ethnomethodology purposefully exclude them. Face-to-face interaction is treated as if it is isolated from the society in which it occurs despite the fact that larger social structures nearly always bear on the interaction in implicit ways. Partial exceptions to be discussed shortly include psychological sociology and ecological psychology which, in a limited way, do bring in macrostructures. In its later versions, symbolic interactionism took a stance in opposition to social structural explanations. Ethnomethodology was specifically launched as an attack on such explanations. Thus, neither of these approaches is capable of dealing with social structures, although in recent years several spokesmen for these approaches have called attention to the necessity for taking them into account (Cicourel, 1981; Knorr-Cetina, 1981; Stryker, 1985). Another important reason for the failure to link social interaction with macrostructures is that the behavior domain typically studied is often one far removed from organizational structures. Although the psychological experiment is typically conducted within a university setting, task-related features of individual behavior rather than the institutional features of the experiment are the focus of study. Similarly, studies of conversation by interactionists or ethnomethodologists typically focus on spontaneous, free exchanges outside of institutional settings.

It might be thought that the topic of socialization, which is central in SSP and which receives some attention in PSP, contradicts this claim. Certainly the family as an institution shapes children's morals, values, attitudes and behaviors; and, in adult socialization, organizations have important effects on individuals' attitudes and behaviors. But our claim is rather that the *ongoing* effects of macrostructures on social interaction are not taken into account in PSP or SSP. Macrostructures often have constraining or facilitating effects on most kinds of social interaction, effects that need to be understood in some detail if social interaction is to be adequately explained.

Despite their neglect, the importance of social structures seems obvious. Knorr-Cetina (1981, p. 12) has put the case in the following way: 'Participants not only routinely transcend the immediate setting by referring to occasions and phenomena at a different time and place, they also continually employ notions and engage in actions whose mutual intelligibility appears to be based upon their presuppositions and knowledge of broader societal institutions.' Since ethnomethodologists, for example, stress the importance of gaining an understanding of the actors' tacit knowledge as well as the conditions underlying social interaction, the analyst must take into account not only social institutions but even those social structures that go unnoticed by the actors.

Symbolic interactionism, PSP, and ethnomethodology are unable to connect the situated action of individuals to the larger society. Yet if institutions and society affect behavior, then at some point their impact on individual actions must be taken into account within any adequate social psychology. The ethnomethodologists deal with this proviso by rejecting any formal social structures that transcend the concrete, situated, everyday activities of individuals. For them, everyday activities are all there are; macrostructures are the fantasies of social theorists. In the unlikely event that they are right, sociology as conventionally practised is not viable. Symbolic interactionists attempt to relate social behavior to macrostructures through the concept of social role. But they reject the Parsonian idea of sets of interlocking roles as constituting social systems or institutions. Instead their concept of role is amorphous: roles are constructed ever anew to fit the situated action of the moment.

Of the several social psychologies, only *psychological sociology* connects individual characteristics to macrostructures. Although Karl Marx is not usually thought of as a social psychologist, his early ideas fit this category. His concept of alienation or alienated labor has 'multiple reference to: (1) social phenomena (states of society, its institutions, rules and norms); (2) individual states of mind (beliefs, desires, attitudes, etc.); (3) a hypothesized empirical relationship between (1) and (2); and (4) a presupposed picture of the "natural" relationship between (1) and (2)' (Lukes, 1967, p. 140, quoted in House, 1977, p. 170).

In his studies of remote villages and mountain pasturelands of the Soviet Union conducted in 1932, Luria (1976) provides a striking example of how larger social structures can affect individual behaviors. Luria observed both underdeveloped illiterate groups and groups involved in modern life affected by the revolution. He describes a part of his results:

> Finally, there are changes in self-awareness of the personality, which advances to the higher level of social awareness and assumes new capabilities for objective, categorical analysis of one's motivation, actions, intrinsic properties, and idiosyncracies. Thus a fact hitherto underrated by psychology becomes apparent: sociohistorical shifts not only introduce new content into the mental world of human beings; they also create new forms of activity and new structures of cognitive functioning. They advance human consciousness to new levels. (quoted in Bronfenbrenner, 1979, pp. 263–4)

Luria's position would imply that the ethnomethodologist's view of practical everyday activity fits best only the more primitive, more uncritical levels of human functioning (for example, the behavior of illiterate peasants). With greater cognitive sophistication, situations perceived to be more regular are more encoded in language and therefore more general; there, the effects of macrostructures become more important. But even among peasants, as we might expect, the authority structures of the larger society have considerable pertinence. Vygotsky (1978) also had a deep appreciation of the relationship between society and human nature. He clearly saw the relationship between society and human characteristics. Over extended periods, the construction of language and an ever more complex, differentiated society acted on humans themselves, changing their activities in profound ways and, as Vygotsky argued, even modified their brains.

More recent research on social structure and personality includes the effect of social stratification on self-image, personality and values; the relation between modernization and personality/behavior, and between urban residence and personality/behavior; the effect of structural relationships of individuals (to teachers, parents and school) upon status attainment; and organizational structures in relation to personality.

Although psychological sociology is sensitive to macrostructures, it is weak on the psychological side. House (1977) observes that the isolation of psychological sociology from the other social psychologies has strengthened it *sociologically* but impoverished it psychologically. He notes that structures are seen as mechanically and mysteriously shaping personality and behavior; microsocial processes that might elaborate our understanding of how this occurs are not investigated. Psychological sociology, then, as defined here, does not adequately tie social psychological processes to macrostructures.

Besides psychological sociology, one relatively small movement within PSP is an exception in giving careful attention to social structures. Roger Barker has spent a lifetime of research on the nature of *behavior settings* and their relation to behavior. This approach has come to be called ecological psychology, and Barker's students are carrying on his work. A behavior setting is a hybrid of features of the physical environment and relevant social structures. Examples are a church, a school, a baseball field. Certainly this focus deals with an important aspect of social psychology; yet, considering the many decades since the approach was initiated, it has failed to have a strong impact on PSP. My suspicion, once again, is that the dominance of the experimental paradigm plus the individual and inward polarities of PSP are responsible for this neglect. One hopeful possibility is that the weakening of these long-standing grounds for PSP will open the way for more intensive work in ecological psychology. In more recent years, work in ecological psychology has been receiving increasing attention (see Stokols, 1977; Wicker, 1979).

In my view, no analysis of social behavior is complete unless it takes into account the ways in which social institutions and other social structures bear on face-to-face situated action. In recognizing larger social structures, one need not deny the reality of agency: individuals can be seen as constructing a social situation while at the same time being constrained by that very situation – as well as by other structures. Giddens (1976, 1979) makes the telling point that 'social structures are both constituted by human agency, and yet at the same time are the very medium of this constitution.' Structures have a duality: they condition social action but at the same time are produced by these very actions. This ongoing process is conditioned in unforeseeable ways by the unintended consequences of previous social actions. For example, the formal structure of language has been created by its use, by people speaking to each other and expressing themselves in writing over long periods of time. Individuals learn to follow the structural patterns of language in speaking or writing, but at times they may create new words and new usages which in turn eventually act back and modify the formal structure of the language.

Structures are not intentional creations; the intentions in acting are subsidiary to the structures themselves, and in some sense structures are unintentional creations. Marriage as an institution has a formal structure, but two people who marry do not intend to recreate or reinforce that structure, but instead marry for quite different reasons. Marriages of the ordinary sort support and maintain that structure. Yet if an appreciable proportion of people marry according to a pattern that deviated from the formal structure, then the structure changes (for instance, if homosexuals marry).

One way to confirm the relevance of social structures to social behavior is to show how social power derived from societal sources actually impacts on the exchange process occurring in face-to-face relationships. Social exchange theory construes all interactions as involving an exchange of costs and benefits between two or more parties, in a manner analogous to economic exchange. What is exchanged is resources that fit the needs of – and so benefit – the parties to the interaction. In addition, the exchange involves some cost to each party. Resources may be psychological attributes, such as physical attractiveness, a sense of humor, empathy and a host of others. Costs include time and effort, but also more psychological effects, such as anxiety, being bored, being criticized and the like. For an attribute of the other party to be a benefit to the first party, the first party must need it. A person who is somewhat depressed may gain a lift through the understanding behavior of another. Or an individual may enjoy the light-hearted humor of another. These examples constitute *mutual* exchanges because the sympathetic or humorous individuals benefit from the response of the other to their sympathy or their humor.

The relation of social psychological processes to macrostructures depends in part on the fact that structural features sometimes determine the resources that different groups of individuals possess. Some people have more powerful resources than others, drawn from societal sources. Similarly, the extent to which certain individuals depend on certain resources is partly shaped by societal structures and processes.

Consider, for example, interactions between men and women. In virtually all societies, men have more power than women, power they derive from the places society accords males. Political and economic power afford clear examples. Such power becomes transmuted into a kind of social power that can be used in face-to-face actions with others, particularly with women. Hence, men have an advantage in interacting with women. Secord (1982) has described this process in some detail, showing how men throughout history have shaped the social roles of women to male advantage. These roles take two basic forms, depending on social power and the sex ratio – the proportion of men to women in the population, itself another 'structural' feature. Scarcity gives a gender some dyadic power – power to negotiate exchanges in face-to-face interactions with the opposite sex (Guttentag and Secord, 1983). But this dyadic power interacts with social power to shape women's roles differently in populations with high or low sex ratios.

When women are scarce, they have dyadic power and men have structural power. Men have to compete with each other to acquire a female partner. Thus it is to the advantage of men who have partners to press for and establish monogamy as a moral imperative, in order to reduce competition from other men. Under those circumstances women are more likely to be satisfied with the domestic role and become politically, economically, and socially less independent. But when women are in oversupply it is no longer to male advantage to reinforce monogamy, and sexual permissiveness becomes the norm. In addition, women now strive for economic and political independence because of their weakness in social exchange: they are doubly disadvantaged in lacking both social power and dyadic power. Since they cannot negotiate favorable relationships with men they need to become more independent.

In sum, this greatly simplified explanation reveals the interplay between male-female interaction on the one hand, and two salient features of the larger society on the other: the superior social power held by men and the variations in the population sex ratio. The effects of the interplay are shown not only in face-to-face interaction, but also in changes in the ratio of illegitimate to legitimate births, in divorce ratios, in sexual morality, and in many other features of human existence. Worth noting is the importance of spelling out precisely how this interplay occurs if changes in interaction and in macrostructures are to be fully understood.

Social psychology and language

All too often, PSP (in particular) is content with identifying variables – abstract categories bereft of social context and richer descriptions of actual action. This impoverishment is intensified by individualistic and inward orientations. Individuals are isolated from the social context, and their internal cognitive states become the principal object of scrutiny. Although everyday behavior is richly impregnated with language, most PSP studies do not permit individuals under observation to speak or write freely, further impoverishing their behavior. To their credit, both the symbolic interactionists and the ethnomethodologists have grasped the importance of language in human action, and it is central in their thinking and their research. Paradoxically, the *social* is almost removed from PSP.

Structuralist-functionalist sociology also suffers when the importance of language for understanding social behavior is stressed. Because of its positivist orientation, this approach often attempts virtually to eliminate ordinary language from behavior descriptions, in favor of more abstract, quantitative characterizations. In the standard view of science, emphasis is placed on objectivity, and language is minimized by making observation physicalistic. Descriptive propositions are somewhat detached from the engaged observer; they become impersonal, factual statements about the observable world. Yet, social behavior is *language-impregnated*; it is not possible to describe social behavior in non-linguistic terms without radically changing its meaning. Moreover, as the ethnomethologists have pointed out, verbal interactions that are observable or recordable are merely the tip of the iceberg; interactions involve the play of a great deal of tacit knowledge and social context that alone make the interaction socially viable. For these reasons, attempts by PSP merely to label complex actions without analysis as 'helping behavior', 'dependent behavior', 'aggressive behavior', and the like, and to use these notions as quantitative variables are apt to transform research into the investigation of something quite different from the action supposedly under actual study. Similarly, choosing a simple act as a dependent variable for inclusion in an experiment and calling it 'aggression' severely limits the investigation of the rich ways in which aggression may be expressed.

Some philosophers it should be noted argue that we cannot have a social *science* unless ordinary language can be eliminated. Rosenberg (1981), a philosopher committed to the standard view, has spelled out the reasons for this in considerable detail. Even though ordinary explanations of human behavior have for thousands of years involved concepts such as belief and desire, and even if some instantiated explanations of actions involving these terms are true, the singular nature of such instances keeps them from making effective contributions to the formation of general laws. Moreover, ordinary language, Rosenberg believes, is hopelessly subjective and thus unsuitable for science. In fact he finds dependence on ordinary language concepts a major reason for the failure of the social sciences. We must stress, of course, that Rosenberg's criticisms are based on his firm belief in the validity of logical empiricism.

Similar views have been expressed by Stich (1983), in his rejection of folk psychology, and his recommendations for a psychology based on a formalized rather than a natural language. Fodor, too, has seen the threat posed by natural language, to his information-processing view of psychology, and has revised his position over the years so as to restrict accounting for action, learning and contentful perception. According to Williams (1985), Fodor has, in his successive publications, recognized the problems posed, for cognitive science, by language and intentional behavior; has progressively restricted the scope of the information-processing paradigm; and has eventually (Fodor, 1983) arrived at the conclusion that the explanatory attempts of cognitive science should be limited to perceptual input and sentence recognition systems.

Although it cannot be argued that the development of a scientific language to replace ordinary language is impossible, it is not clear that such an accomplishment would provide the kinds of explanation needed. Even though ordinary language is occasionally enriched by adopting technical psychological terms, no comprehensive scientific language for describing behavior has yet emerged, or is it likely to. Harré and Secord (1972), for example, argue that any application of social science must necessarily involve ordinary language. The behaviors or actions of people must necessarily be described in ordinary language terms simply because behavior itself is inextricably entangled in language forms. Mere motion in space is seldom of interest to anyone; when movements are expressive, their meaning can only be understood in language terms. Moreover, most human interaction is fully linguistic in character and, although it is embellished by nonlinguistic features such as expressive movements, voice inflections, facial expressions and the like, the action would be severely underdescribed if its linguistic features were ignored. The very fabric of society as well as the meanings of everyday behaviors are woven into ordinary language. Thus to describe behaviors in a nonlinguistic fashion is to emphasize the asocial features of behavior and really fail to study its more regnant social forms. The ultimate paradox is that *social* pyschologists are often guilty of adopting this myopic orientation.

This is not to say that a technically specialized, novel language could not provide *part* of a scientific explanation. An overall explanation may well involve neuropsychological terms as well as terms used to identify abstractly theoretical social structures quite unfamiliar at the level of natural social behavior. The claim, rather, is that the social behavior must itself must be describable in ordinary language terms or, at the very least, any scientific language describing and explaining social behavior must be paraphrasable into, or systematically linked to, ordinary lan-guuage terms. Failing that, the target behavior could not be understood.

Another much contested way of expressing the significance of language for understanding human behavior is reflected in the idea that action is to be explained, not (or not just) in terms of antecedent causes, but in terms of reasons or accounts that justify the action. A. R. Louch's (1966) views are representative of one branch of this philosophical position. Louch takes the extreme position that neither a science of human action nor of society is possible. His reasons are instructive. Human action is only explained, he argues, through what he calls 'moral' appraisal. By this he means that actions are explained when the situation or circumstances are seen as entitling the action. We say that a person's anger or fear are explained when the situation and circumstances call for such emotional responses. Such accounts are not limited to those that the actor can provide; sometimes an observer can explain an act in a way the actor cannot; at other times, the actor might provide an account only in retrospect, or might come to accept an account only after extended negotiation with others.

Harré and Secord (1972) offer an approach called *ethogeny*, which takes a less extreme position and does not reject the idea of a human science, but which places great emphasis on accounts as forms of explanation. The profound significance of explanatory accounts that entitle particular actions is typically missed by psychologists and social scientists whose thinking is grounded in logical empiricism. Perhaps this is because they assimilate such accounts to 'introspective reports', 'verbal reports', 'subjective reports', or 'phenomenological reports'. For them, these reports are *data* from which the scientist draws inferences that help to provide a scientific explanation of the action under study. They fail to grasp that such reports are *not* data, but the actor's *interpretations* of the action at issue – possibly, then, data at one remove. These interpretations have a status similar to the scientist's interpretation. Neither the scientist nor the actor has ultimate authority. Sometimes the scientist's interpretation may be superior because of greater experience with the action under study or because of observations to which he or she has privileged access. But also possibly, the actor has privileged or tacit knowledge of private feelings or thoughts that afford a more correct perspective than the scientist's. For an adequate science, these dual interpretations must be reconciled; social scientists cannot assume that *their* description provides a true account of what actually happened.

In concluding his superb review of observational methods, Weick (1985) emphasizes this duality. He warns that observers doing field studies must not repeat the arrogance of the experimental social psychologist confined within his or her laboratory. Weick marks that arrogance most effectively, in three steps:

1 The observer treats the observer's version of a participant's life as that person's real life.
2 The participant's version of that same life is treated as the subjective view of what 'actually' happened.
3 The observer accomodates these two versions by explaining the processes that cause the participant to experience the life (version 2) other than the way it *actually* happened (version 1).

In other words, instead of taking the participant's version seriously, the experimenter explains it away by invoking processes that label the participant's version as a distortion of what 'actually happened'.

Actions are explained in terms of accounts only when careful observation and description detail background considerations and the circumstances of an action in such a manner as to show that the action was called for or justified – or invites questions of justification. The contrast with a positivistic stance could not be more pronounced. Action follows not from antecedent *causes* and not in a mechanical fashion, but comes about because of the nature of persons and the circumstances in which they find themselves. Within this perspective it is extremely difficult to reduce the action to dependent variables or the situation and circumstances to independent variables. Explaining action is not so much a matter of correlation between such variables as it is a rational demonstration that, given the circumstances, the action that took place was justified or entitled (or pertinently not).

The link between this philosophical perspective and ethnomethodology is very close, even if it has not been explicitly recognized by either party. Ethnomethdologists emphasize that action can never be completely described without a thorough consideration of the tacit knowledge possessed by the actor and the circumstances associated with the action. For them, *any* action is problematic, in that actors must themselves participate in a process of making sense of the situation and construing actions appropriately as they interact. This orientation complements and fits in closely with the notion of actions as entitled or justified by the situation. The latter philosophical notion, though, perhaps more than ethnomethodology, brings out the evaluative, appraising character of the process of describing human action.

What underlies both perspectives is an appeal to rules or conventions, sometimes encapsulated into roles. Roles are normative and involve consensus across a wide spectrum of society. Everyone understands the fury of a husband upon discovering that his wife has been unfaithful. But the ethnomethodologists in particular stress tacit practical rules that help individuals in interaction to put a construction on the local situation. They make much of the idiosyncratic nature of situations and the repeated reconstruction of their meanings in new forms from day to day. Here, certain rules are invoked to help explain how actors do this work in their daily encounters. Interpretations may be based on a kind of informal logic, as in 'An eye for an eye and a tooth for a tooth'. Social exchange theory, which involves maximizing one's rewards and minimizing one's costs, is another candidate for providing heuristic explanations of how participants in interaction manage their daily encounters, although it is used in PSP and not in ethnomethodology.

A caveat should be inserted here. As Weick (1985, vol. 1, p. 574) observes, citing none other than Erving Goffman, the idea that reality is socially constructed can be overdone. The famous dictum of W. I. Thomas, 'If men define situations as real, they are real in their consequences', can be carried too far. A person who imagines a tiger lurking behind a bush might freeze with fear or might run, but will not be eaten, no matter how vivid the fantasy. A great many situations are not enigmatic but routine; moreover their settings may be quite fixed. For regular churchgoers, there is little that is ambiguous about a church service. Garfinkel's (1967) claim that the indexicality of situations is *awesome* may apply in some cases, but surely not in all.

Philosophers and others who argue that explaining human action should feature situational entitlement and the nature of the person or agent inolved often reject the possibility of a science of psychology or sometimes reject altogether the possibility of any social science. The ethogenic approach as originally introduced by Harré and Secord (1972) takes a less radical position. Explaining human action in terms of accounts does not preclude the possibility of causal analysis. Not only are reasons sometimes causes, but neurophysiological as well as psychological constructs may play a causal role in explanation. As developed further by Harré and his colleagues, however, ethogeny seems to have narrowed its focus and to be offered as an alternative to PSP and especially to experimentation as a method (Harré 1979, 1983, also this volume).

The currrent practices of some ethogenists have much in common with ethnomethodology; both reject the experiment on the grounds that it cannot possibly deal with the rich background and contextual circumstances that surround human action. Yet, what seems to be rejected, perhaps with good reason, is a kind of narrow prototype of the experiment, a rejection that hardly does justice to the wide variety of methods used in laboratory and field experiments. In fact, the term *experiment* is used very loosely in social psychology to include studies that merely vary a set of conditions in a field situation in order to observe their effect on the actions that occur. There is nothing to prohibit experimenters working within this broader concept from dealing with participants in ways compatible with ethnomethodology and ethogeny. As a matter of fact, a group of social psychologists, mostly in Great Britain, have been strongly influenced by ethogeny and are doing research under the rubric of *situated action*, but accept the experiment as one of several methodological approaches (Ginsburg, 1979; Ginsburg, Brenner, and von Cranach, 1985). Their ideas and methods are very close to the position originally laid out in Harré and Secord (1972).

Another encouraging trend suggesting recognition of the arguments offered by ethnomethodologists falls under the rubric of social constructionism (Gergen and Davis, 1985). Investigators to whom this term may be applied are carrying out descriptive, ethogenic, hermeneutic, analytic, historical and ethnomethodological research and come from all the social science disciplines except economics. Their philosophy is anti-positivist and they especially recognize the indexicality of social interaction.

In the newly released third edition of the *Handbook of Social Psychology*, Aronson, Brewer and Carlsmith (1985), in their authoritative chapter on experimentation in social psychology, freely acknowledge the persistent criticisms of experiment occurring during the 17-year span since the second edition. The authors describe the basic dilemma of the experimental social psychologist as follows. Participants must be deeply involved in the experimental task, lest the results be banal. Yet producing the realism that engenders involvement means that the experience will be complex and lead to 'great difficulty in understanding precisely what actually constitutes the experimental treatment' (p. 476). The result is a loss of experimental control. But the dilemma is not a fatal one, and the authors note many important changes in the research literature that mute many of the criticisms of PSP.

Besides meeting ethical concerns, new lines of experimentation are emerging. Many experiments are 'judgment experiments', in which participants are asked to recognize, recall, classify or evaluate stimulus materials presented. In effect, these participants are treated as *observers*. More experiments than was the case two decades ago, although still a small minority, are being conducted in field settings. Most especially, the authors acknowledge the importance of having participants interpret events in the same way that the experimenter does, and provide suggestions as to how this might be accomplished in laboratory settings. Special attention is given to certain aspects of the experiment as a social situation: for example, the necessity of insuring that participants fully understand the instructions given, and the necessity of conducting long, probing interviews in connection with pretesting the experimental treatment. Also, more emphasis is placed on clarifying the dependent behavior under study. A thorough briefing is recommended, and enlisting the participant's aid in critcizing and improving the experiment is considered desirable. The importance of programmatic research involving a line of varied experiments addressed to the same issues is stressed as a counter to the criticism of the isolated experiment.

Taking a cue from this last point, we may note that a review of the research literature in almost any active domain in social psychology suggests that the rejection of whole lines of research just because they are primarily experimental is unwarranted. For example, in the last two decades or so, over 1,000 studies of helping behavior have been conducted by social psychologists (Dovidio, 1984). Although most of these have been laboratory studies, it would be churlish and silly to argue that this prodigious output has not increased our understanding of helping behavior. Not only have we learned of circumstantial or situational conditions that facilitate or inhibit helping behavior, but we have acquired more insight into the psychological dynamics of being confronted with a situation involving a victim who needs help and how pertinent factors lead to action or inaction on the part of the bystander. In many of these studies, participants find themselves in situations involving a victim in distress – that arises naturally rather than in a contrived way; so that the usual objections to treating the experiment as itself a social situation need not always apply.

It is clear that asking people how they might react to various situations involving victims in distress would be totally inadequate on the grounds that their anticipations would be unreliable. On the other hand, intensive, probing discussions with participants who have just been in such situations might well enrich our knowledge. Such inquiry could be enhanced if video technology were used to replay the scene while questioning the participants concerning their action sequences.

Despite the gains made in understanding helping behavior, limitations remain. Worth observing is the fact that the dependent act under study has usually been focused in terms of bystander intervention rather than in terms of the character of the helping behavior itself – a fact that Dovidio (1984) himself notes in his review. Bystander intervention is the simple act of moving to help or refraining from doing so – an act that requires little analysis and which is identified minimally in the answer to the question, 'Did he?' or Didn't he?' Dovidio also brings to our attention the fact that experimental studies of helping in contrived situations cannot inform us of naturally occurring *rates* of helpfulness in life situations; and he also notes that the dominance of the experimental paradigm has even shaped the questions that are asked in field studies, thus artificially limiting the scope of these studies. Moreover, only a handful of studies of helping behavior concern acquaintances or friends, despite the probability that help occurs more frequently in such relationships. That such limitations remain after more than 1,000 studies of helping behavior reflects the power of the dominant PSP paradigm to constrain inquiry.

Coda

Looking back over the emergence of various approaches to social psychology, we see that two themes especially stand out. One is the waxing and waning of logical positivism/empiricism and its association with the rise of experimental social psychology and structural functionalism in sociology – followed by critical attacks on these paradigms and the emergence of such counterapproaches as symbolic interactionism, ethnomethodology, ethogeny and social constructivism (along with dialectics and hermeneutics, which have not been discussed for lack of space). These contrasting paradigms have in common a protest against positivism and an emphasis on the necessity of taking into account language and associated subjective features of the human condition. Taken together, they offer a powerful critique of social psychology as it has been practised in the past. Although many social psychologists continue to forge ahead along old pathways, as if they were wearing horse blinders, others (in increasing numbers) are trying to remedy the worst excesses of positivism/empiricism. It is likely that future generations of social psychologists will have markedly different views from those that have prevailed earlier.

The other theme is the vigor and sheer diversity of the various independent approaches to social psychology. Experimental social psychology has made many valuable contributions. It has also strongly resisted criticism and toally ignored sociological social psychology. The other approaches discussed here have been equally vigorous and resistant to criticism. I cannot but reflect on the relevance of this to scientific inquiry. Kuhn's (1970) notion of paradigms comes to mind, but certain re-emphases are indicated. The idea that a whole community of scientists shares a paradigmatic set of assumptions and practices certainly does not apply to social psychologists, let alone psychologists or sociologists. What seems more characteristic is that these disciplines are sharply divided into subsets whose proponents share a paradigm unique to their subset. Moreover, what seems especially crucial in every case is that they share a unique exemplar – a way of doing research that is treated almost as a magical device for solving scientific puzzles and insuring fruitful results. Quite possibly, this semi-religious devotion to an exemplar and its associated paradigmatic beliefs is a necessary prerequisite for advancing scientific knowledge.

A final observation is in order. Although insulated paradigmatic efforts often are creative, they are by themselves seldom useful in applying the social sciences to the solution of social problems. Most social problems require a breadth of knowledge, not narrowness. Typically, only interdisciplinary efforts are adequate. Applications of science to social problems require a great deal of knowledge that extends beyond any narrow paradigm and beyond science itself. The interconnectedness of social life signifies that various behaviors are facilitated or discouraged by social structural factors that must be accommodated as well as taken into account. Thus, if a mature science is to be socially useful, it must transcend competing paradigms by developing theory that embraces them despite their apparent incongruence, and it must be in touch at a tacit level with effective social structures that theory may not yet have grasped.

REFERENCES

Abelson, R. P., Aronson, E., McGuire, W. J., et al. (eds) 1968: *Theories of Cognitive Consistency: a sourcebook.* Chicago: Rand McNally.
Allport, F. H. 1924: *Social Psychology.* Boston: Houghton Mifflin.
Allport, G. W. 1954: The historical background of modern social psychology. In G. Lindzey (ed.), *Handbook of Social Psychology, vol. 1. Theory and Methods,* 2nd edition, Cambridge, Mass.: Addison-Wesley.
Aronson, E., Brewer, M., Carlsmith, J. M. 1985: Experimentation in social

psychology. in G. Lindzey and E. Aronson (eds), *Handbook of Social Psychology, vol. 1. Theory and Methods*, 3rd edition, New York: Random House.

Bhaskar, R. 1975: *A Realist Theory of Science*. Leeds: Leeds Books. (An edition published in 1978 by Harvester Press contains a postscript clarifying Bhaskar's use of the term 'law'.)

Bhaskar, R. 1978: On the possibility of social scientific knowledge and the limits of behaviorism. *Journal for the Theory of Social Behaviour*, 8, 1–28.

Bhaskar, R. 1979: *The Possibility of Naturalism*. Brighton, Sussex: Harvester Press.

Blumer, H. 1969: *Symbolic Interactionism: perspective and method*. Englewood Cliffs, NJ: Prentice Hall.

Bronfenbrenner, U. 1979. *The Ecology of Human Development: experiments by nature and design*. Cambridge, Mass.: Harvard University Press.

Brown, H. I. 1977: *Perception, Theory and Commitment*. Chicago, Ill.: University of Chicago Press.

Cicourel, A. V. 1969: Basic and normative rules in the negotiation of status and role. In D. Sudnow (ed.), *Studies in Interaction*, New York: Free Press.

Cicourel, A. V. 1981: Notes on the integration of micro- and macro-levels of analysis. In K. Knorr-Cetina, and A. V. Cicourel (eds), *Advances in Social Theory and Methodology*, London: Routledge and Kegan Paul.

Cooley, C. H. 1902: *Human Nature and the Social Order*. New York: Charles Scribner's Sons.

Douglas, J. D. 1967: *The Social Meaning of Suicide*. Princeton, NJ: Princeton University Press.

Dovidio, J. F. 1984: Helping behavior and altruism: An empirical and conceptual overview. In L. Berkowitz (ed.), *Advances in Experimental Social Psychology*, vol. 17, New York: Academic Press.

Durkheim, E. 1895: *The Rules of Sociological Method*. 8th edition, translated by S. A. Solovay and J. H. Mueller, Edited by G. E. G. Catlin. London: Collier-Macmillan, 1938.

Festinger, L. 1957: *A Theory of Cognitive Dissonance*. New York: Harper and Row.

Fodor, J. A. 1983: *The Modularity of Mind*. Cambridge, Mass.: MIT Press.

Garfinkel, H. 1967: *Studies in Ethnomethodology*. Englewood Cliffs, NJ: Prentice Hall.

Gergen, K. J., and Davis, K. E. (eds) 1985: *The Social Construction of the Person*. New York: Springer-Verlag.

Giddens, A. 1976: *New Rules of Sociological Method*. London: Hutchinson.

Giddens, A. 1979: *Central Problems in Social Theory*. London: Macmillan.

Ginsburg, G. P. 1979: *Emerging Strategies in Social Psychological Research*. Beverly Hills, Cal.: Sage Publications.

Ginsburg, G. P., Brenner, M. and von Cranach, M. 1985: *Discovery Strategies in the Psychology of Action*. London: Academic Press.

Guttentag, M., and Secord, P. F. 1983: *Too Many Women? The sex ratio question*. Beverley Hills, Cal.: Sage Publications.

Harré, R. 1970: *The Principles of Scientific Thinking*. Chicago, Ill.: University of Chicago Press.

Harré, R. 1979: *Social Being: a theory for social psychology*. Oxford: Basil Blackwell.

Harré, R. 1983: *Personal Being: a theory for individual psychology*. Oxford: Basil Blackwell.

Harré, R., and Secord, P. F. 1972: *The Explanation of Social Behavior*. Oxford: Basil Blackwell.

Heider, F. 1958: *The Psychology of Interpersonal Relations*. New York: John Wiley.

Hempel, C. G. 1963: *Aspects of Scientific Explanation*. New York: Free Press.

House, J. S. 1977: The Three Faces of Social Psychology. *Sociometry: a journal of research in social psychology*, 40, 161–77.

Knorr-Cetina, K. 1981: Introduction: The micro-sociological challenge of macro-sociology. In K. Knorr-Cetina and A. V. Cicourel (eds), *Advances in Social Theory and Methodology*, London: Routledge and Kegan Paul.

Kuhn, T. S. 1970: *The Structure of Scientific Revolutions*, 2nd edition. Chicago, Ill.: University of Chicago Press.

Layder, D. 1981: *Structure, Interaction and Social Theory*. London: Routledge and Kegan Paul.

Lewin, K., Lippit, R. and White, R. 1939: Patterns of aggressive behavior in experimentally created social climates. *Journal of Social Psychology*, 10, 271–99.

Likert, R. 1932: A technique for the measurement of attitudes. *Archives of Psychology*, Columbia University, No. 140.

Louch, A. R. 1966: *Explanation and Human Action*. Oxford: Basil Blackwell.

Lukes, S. 1967: Alienation and anomie. In P. Laslett and W. Runciman (eds), *Philosophy, Politics and Society. 3rd series*, Oxford: Basil Blackwell.

Luria, A. R. 1976: *Cognitive Development: its cultural and social foundations*. Cambridge, Mass.: Harvard Unversity Press.

Mead, G. H. 1934: *Mind, Self, and Society: from the standpoint of a social behaviorist*. Chicago, Ill.: University of Chicago Press.

Parsons, T. 1981: *The Social System*. New York: Free Press.

Rosenberg, A. 1981: *Sociobiology and the Preemption of Social Science*. Baltimore: Johns Hopkins University Press.

Scheffler, I. 1967: *Science and Subjectivity*. New York: Bobbs-Merrill.

Schutz, A. J. 1962: *Collected Papers I: The Problem of Social Reality*, edited by Maurice Natanson. The Hague: Martinus Nijhoff.

Schutz, A. J. 1964: *Collected Papers II: Studies in Social Theory*, edited by A. Brockersen. The Hague: Martinus Nijhoff.

Schutz, A. J. 1966: *Collected Papers III: Studies in Phenomenological Philosophy*, edited by I. Schutz. The Hague: Martinus Nijhoff.

Secord, P. F. 1982: The origin and maintenance of social roles: the case of sex roles. In W. Ickes and E. S. Knowles (eds), *Personality, Roles, and Social Behavior*, New York: Springer-Verlag.

Secord, P. F., and Backman, C. W. 1964: *Social Psychology*. New York: McGraw-Hill Book Co.

Steiner, I. D. 1974: Whatever happened to the group in social psychology? *Jouurnal of Experimental Social Psychology*, 10, 94–108.

Stich, S. P. 1983: *From Folk Psychology to Cognitive Science: the case against belief*. Cambridge Mass.: MIT Press.

Stokols, D. (ed.) 1977: *Perspectives on Environment and Behavior*. New York: Plenum.

Stryker, S., and Statham, A. 1985: Symbolic interaction and role theory. In E. Aronson, M. Brewer, and J. M. Carlsmith (eds), *Handbook of Social Psychology. vol. 1: Theory and Methods*, 3rd edition, New York: Random House.

Sumner, W. G. 1906: *Folkways: a study of the sociological importance of usages, manners, customs, mores, and morals*. New York: Dover Publications.

Suppe, F. (ed.) 1977: *The Structure of Scientific Theories*, 2nd edition. Urbana, Ill.: University of Illinois Press.

Thomas, W. I., and Znaniecki, F. 1918: *The Polish Peasant in Europe and America*. 5 vols. Boston: Badger.

Thurstone, L. L. 1928: Attitudes can be measured. *American Journal of Sociology*, 33, 529–54.

Triplett, N. 1897: The dynamogenic factors in pacemaking and competition. *American Journal of Psychology*, 9, 507–33.

Vygotsky, L. S. 1978: *Mind in Society: the development of higher psychological processes*. Cambridge, Mass. and London: Harvard University Press.

Watkins, J. W. N. 1959: Historical explanation in the social sciences. In P. Gardiner (ed.), *Theories of History*, New York: Free Press.

Weick, K. E. 1985: Systematic observational methods. In G. Lindzey and Elliott Aronson (eds), *Handbook of Social Psychology, vol 1. Theory and Methods*, 3rd edition, New York: Random House.

Wicker, A. W. 1979: *An Introduction to Ecological Psychology*. Monterey, Cal.: Brooks-Cole.

Williams, M. 1985: Wittgenstein's rejection of scientific psychology. *Journal for the Theory of Social Behavior*, 15, 203–23.

Index